AFRICAN TRADITIONAL RELIGION

EDITOR:

THE REV. PROFESSOR E. O. JAMES

D.LITT., PH.D., F.S.A., HON. D.D.

Professor of the History and Philosophy of Religion in the University of London

AFRICAN TRADITIONAL RELIGION

by

GEOFFREY PARRINDER
M.A., D.D., PH.D.

SENIOR LECTURER IN RELIGIOUS STUDIES,
UNIVERSITY COLLEGE, IBADAN, NIGERIA

GREENWOOD PRESS, PUBLISHERS
WESTPORT, CONNECTICUT

Originally published in 1954
by Hutchinson's University Library

Library of Congress Catalogue Card Number 75-100215

SBN 8371-3401-3

PRINTED IN UNITED STATES OF AMERICA

CONTENTS

INTRODUCTION

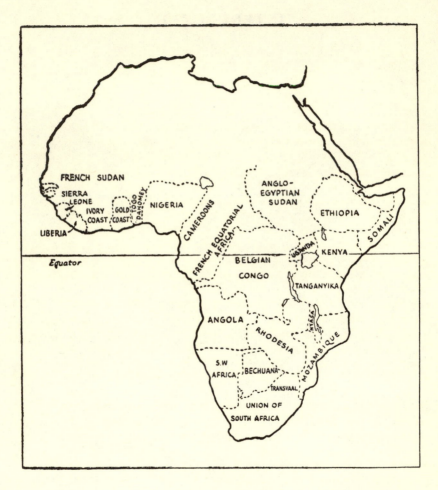

THE SIGNIFICANCE OF AFRICAN RELIGION

EMIL LUDWIG is reported to have asked once when on a visit to Africa, "How can the untutored African conceive God?" The same question may occur to the general reader. This reader may have some knowledge of the religions of other continents, especially Asia, and know that Hinduism, Buddhism and Islam are great faiths, with a long history, considerable literature, and innumerable temples and priests. But what is there comparable in Africa, and of what importance is it?

Africa is receiving much more attention today than hitherto. No longer is it called the Dark Continent. Britain is the mother-country of a great commonwealth, though some Britons seem hardly to realize this fact and look on coloured people with suspicion. Most of the crown colonies are in Africa, and Nigeria, where this book was written, is the largest crown colony of all. Whatever happens in Africa today may be of importance to the whole commonwealth: a mixed marriage in Bechuanaland, a royal funeral in the Gold Coast, a secret society in Kenya, affect people far beyond the countries where these things take place.

The African peoples are pressing on towards taking a greater share in the government of their own lands. The colonial governments are trying to ride on top of the wave, but their success or failure depends upon a close understanding of the peoples they govern. It is "an age of transition", blessed phrase. From afar we watch the rapid changes. How can they be understood, and their future predicted or controlled? What are the forces behind these surging peoples of Africa?

One of the greatest forces has ever been the power of religion. "This incurably religious people", is a phrase often on the lips of many old African administrators. Religion still wields great power in the modern world, whether it be a Mahdi of

9

the Sudan, or the 800 odd sects of South Africa. Not only gods but spiritual forces of many kinds are very potent: witness the lucky charms which most babies and many adults wear, the libations made to the spirits at the crises of life, the oaths supported by spiritual sanctions, the witch-hunts that are still so frequent and distressing.

Of course, Emil Ludwig's phrase "the untutored African" is out of date, if it was ever applicable, for all peoples have some traditions and skill if not book-learning. Today very many Africans are reaching a high level of education, millions have become Christian or Muslim, and religious loyalties change with other customs. But not only do the majority of Africans still hold to the traditional religion of their fathers, but also behind the veneer of the new beliefs of most educated people lie older ideas that will not disappear for a long time yet. This is only to be expected, since Europe still retains ancient pagan notions, albeit somewhat baptized, despite the thousand years and more of Christianity. To Africans, the spiritual world is so real and near, its forces intertwining and inspiring the visible world that, whether pagan or Christian, man has to reckon with "things invisible to mortal sight".

Amid the more than 138,000,000 people of Africa, however, there must be great diversity of religion. Can one compare this with Hinduism or Islam? The desert nomad of Somaliland has little in common with the citizen of Dakar who knows no language but French, and the Cow Fulani of Nigeria must have a very different mentality from the miner of the Rand. Lacking a governing organization how can one speak at all usefully of African religion?

Firstly, the homogeneity of other religions is much less real than apparent. The central organizations of European Christianity are quite exceptional. Hinduism, of course, is a medley of ascetic philosophy and popular polytheism. But Islam also, for all its apparently uniform worship, has its "Two-and-seventy jarring sects"; and the mystical Persian Sufi is far removed from the fanatical Senussi of Cyrenaica. Even in Christianity there is a vast difference in outlook and worship between the Maronite of Lebanon and the Quaker of England or the Adventist of America.

THE SIGNIFICANCE OF AFRICAN RELIGION   11

Secondly, there is much more kinship between the various peoples of Africa than might appear at first sight. Anthropologists have written many monographs on different African peoples, and because little has been done so far to collate and compare their findings, the notion is abroad that every African tribe is very peculiar if not unique. But the resemblances are far more important than the differences. Dr. Hilda Kuper, a great authority on South Africa, has said, "The piling up of ethnographic detail produces an impression of chaos where there is in fact only variation on a few themes. African societies can be broadly classified into a limited number of economic and political types and the difference between the most varied African tribes is slight when compared with the difference between the most highly specialized African society and developed industrial societies. By comparison, African tribal societies are relatively undifferentiated and homogeneous."[1]

This great comparative homogeneity of African society is apparent in the religious sphere. Ethnically the tropical and south African peoples are roughly divided between the Sudanese negroes of West Africa and the Bantu of Central and South Africa; with some Hamites or Half-Hamites in East Central and Hottentots in South-West Africa. But in religious beliefs there is great similarity between many parts of the continent that cuts across racial origins perhaps because of contacts over the centuries. Thus a Supreme Being is worshipped both by Ashanti in the west and Kikuyu in the east, there are divine kings in Nigeria and Uganda, witches in Dahomey and Bechuanaland, a dowry system in the Ivory Coast and Basutoland, female circumcision in the Gold Coast and among the Half-Hamitic Masai, niche burial for Hottentots and Yoruba. Worship of nature gods is a feature of West Africa, but by no means all of it, for it is as lacking in Sierra Leone as in the Transvaal.

We shall try, then, to treat African religion on a comparative basis, gathering material from various parts of the continent. The broad lines of religious belief will be sketched. For details the student must go to the studies of anthropologists. No history or description of any religion can hope to do

[1] *The Listener*, 21st August, 1952.

more than show the main tendencies, and this is enough for the general reader.

Africa South of the Sahara

To be of any use the study needs delimitation. One can no longer wave a hand and say, in the manner of Livingstone, "consider Africa". From the seventh century of our era Islam spread across North Africa, and later down into the Sudan and the east and west coasts. We shall not deal with Islam and its conversions, except incidentally to illustrate the medley of modern faiths. Roughly, Africa south of the Sahara is to be our field of study; from Sierra Leone in the west to the Nuba mountains in the east, and down to the Cape in the south. This is a vast enough area, without attempting somehow to squeeze in North Africa and Egypt, so different from the equatorial and southern peoples and regions.

Over most of this area Christianity too has sent its missions, and there are numerous Christians, from the tiny handful in Swaziland to the majority in Uganda. Despite its phenomenal success, Christianity is still a minority movement in most places although often comprising the educated minority. Moreover, the best studies of African peoples, when they describe the religion, deal almost exclusively with the ancient and pagan beliefs. This is of great historical importance, and, while modern religion may be changing, these studies enable us to understand the background of faith which still influences most men today.

On the peoples of tropical and southern Africa there has been appearing since the First World War a steadily increasing flow of serious works, the products of years of intensive research. Long and detailed monographs deal with every part of the social life of some large and some quite obscure tribes. Recently a series of Ethnographic Surveys, published by the International African Institute, has extended and summarized much of our knowledge. These studies are invaluable to the student, but they are much too long, detailed and expensive for the general reader. A short, comparative, and not exhaustive account is what is presented to him here.

It will be evident that one writer cannot hope to visit all

the places he mentions, let alone have a knowledge of their languages which are as diverse as Babel. It is probably more profitable to live for years in a few regions, and gradually to absorb as much as one can of the local ways of thought. Then one is better armed for a study of the larger field. This is what I have done, and I do not pretend to have unearthed much new material, any more than a writer on the general aspects of Buddhism would make such a claim. This is a general comparative study to serve as an introduction; the professional anthropologist must not seek here what it is never intended to give.

Of the importance of the religious life of Africa there is no doubt. The European at home cannot understand much of his African news without some sketch of African religion. The European in Africa, so often fond of dogmatizing about "knowing the native mind", cannot possibly do so without approaching the religion in the right way. The modern African himself has not infrequently been taught to misunderstand the religion of his ancestors, so that it comes as a surprise to him to learn that their beliefs can be studied fairly and even with sympathy. Further, there is observable today a tendency for some Africans to glorify their largely uncharted past, and to dogmatize about some respectable ancestry for it in Egypt or even Mesopotamia. Here again, correct knowledge is more important than theory.

Old Versions of African Religion

It is probably true to say that African religion has been more misunderstood, and has suffered more at the hands of the early writers, than any other part of African life. Unhappily old misconceptions linger with us still.

It is not so much that the old writers were all of them bad observers. Indeed some of them did make good use of the unique opportunities they had of seeing rites that have now practically disappeared. But the rather depreciatory language which they often used, and the semi-humorous attitude many of them took up, has infected succeeding generations.

Father Merolla wrote of a ceremony of the Loango in the seventeenth century, "I saw likewise at a distance an oath administered, which that it might be done with the greater efficacy, it was proposed to be taken in the presence of their idol: this hobgoblin resembled in some measure a mountebank's merry-andrew, having a divers coloured vest on, and a red cap on its head."

William Bosman, a Dutch traveller to the Guinea Coast in the early eighteenth century, writes in this strain of what he calls the "false gods" of the country: "God, say they, commits the Government of the world to their Idols; to whom as the second, third and fourth persons distant in degree from God, and our lawful Governors, we are obliged to apply ourselves. . . . It is really the more to be lamented that the negroes idolize such worthless Nothings by reason that several amongst them have no very unjust idea of the Deity." And again he imports a European theological idea into his description of a ceremony by saying, "The Devil is annually banished from all their towns with an abundance of Ceremony, at an appointed time set apart for that end."

Sir Richard Burton in 1864 can hardly restrain himself from an amused scepticism. "The African—somewhat like the vulgar Asiatic and European, especially the southern—holds the illogical belief that his dark, silent, eternal Deity can be influenced by intercessions animate and inanimate, human and bestial; that the leopard and the crocodile, like the wali (saint) and the prophet, and that the fetish shrub, like the Salagram, the Karabela clay, or the bite of True Cross, may, by some inexplicable process, control the inscrutable course of mundane law."

But it is shocking to find a modern globe-trotter writing of the realm of the Rain-queen of the Lovedu as "built up on immorality, deceit and crime, with no effective striking force to support it." And he depicts the queen as surrounded by attractive girls whose task is to lure neighbouring chiefs and "to induce their new masters to attend the festivities, dances, beer drinks, orgies, licentious debaucheries continuously held at the rain-priestess' capital." Fortunately we now have the Kriges' careful study of the social and religious pattern of this rain-queen's kingdom to rebut such fanciful assertions.

One might quote almost endlessly, but these specimens will suggest how hard it has been for Europeans to treat African religious beliefs seriously, and how vague and misleading terminology has been in the past.

"Fetish" and "Juju"

One thing that clearly emerges is the necessity of using more precise terms than in the past, and of abandoning some of the older words as absolutely devoid of any consistent meaning.

The word "fetishism" has long been used as a rough description of the religion of much of Africa, and it is still to be found though much criticized. The fact is that it is a thoroughly unsatisfactory word, and it gives a distorted and unfair picture of the religion of the African peoples.

The word was introduced by the Portuguese, who were the first and for long the chief traders along the western and equatorial coast of Africa. They saw Africans wearing charms and amulets, and they called them *feitiço*. As Fowler says, "Though it has the air of a mysterious barbarian word, it is in reality the same as *factitious* and means (like an idol, the work of men's hands) a made thing." From Portuguese it came into French and English, and used to be spelt fetiche or fetish, but the latter spelling has now prevailed.

If this word were only confined to magical charms that would not be unsuitable, but the trouble is that it is used for religious objects and practices far beyond these limits, and it also isolates African practices (as if they were purely negro and exotic) from similar ones to be found all over the world.

Old Bosman said, "They cry out, Let us make Fetiche; by which they express as much as, let us perform our religious worship." But one is surprised to find Sir James Frazer in our own century speaking of "the fetish king of Western Africa", when he means a religious head as distinct from a civil ruler. And Mary Kingsley, although she began to get troubled because the word fetish "is getting very loosely used in England", yet went on to say, "When I say Fetish or JuJu, I mean the religion of the natives of West Africa."

Now the religion of African peoples is not just the worship or the use of the work of men's hands. It is known today that no "heathen in his blindness bows down to wood and stone". The "heathen" worships a spiritual being, who may be approached through a material object. But all Africans believe that there are other spiritual forces than those associated with "idols". The great Creator has very few temples or images, but is almost everywhere believed in. Many other gods and ancestors are prayed to without any material representation of them being used.

Other writers are even more careless. Nassau, a missionary writer on Central Africa, used the word fetish so widely that he even wrote of a "fetish prayer". Monteiro, writing on the Congo, spoke of "undergoing fetish" as taking an oath. And across the other side of the continent Roscoe uses fetish of the Baganda emblems of gods, of medicinal preparations, and of "a fetish of herbs" used by an army on the warpath.

Clearly a word that has such various uses is of little scientific value. It is often, at the least, positively misleading. For this reason Rattray in the Gold Coast, and some modern anthropologists, have tried to restrict the use of the word fetish solely to "charms, amulets, talismans, mascots". But why not use these very words? And, as already pointed out, such a restriction would isolate African practices from the rest of the world, and it is most undesirable to perpetuate such a false antithesis.

It is evident that fetish is a most ambiguous word and the time has come for all serious writers and speakers to abandon it completely and finally. Furthermore, the French have extensive interests in Africa, and they use "fetiche" to denote the gods and their symbols, which Rattray and some English writers would expressly exclude from this category. The "charms, amulets, and talismans" are represented in French by "grisgris". The latter word also occurs rarely in English. John Barbot said in the seventeenth century, "Grigri are little square leather bags, in which are inclos'd some folded pieces of written paper . . . being in the nature of spells". The French dictionary calls grisgris a "protective amulet". Confusion worse confounded. Why cannot we use straightforward European terms, in which our languages are not poor? It is better to use well-established self-evident terms in translation, rather than words which may have a mysterious barbarian air but are in reality nothing of the sort.

The same applies to "Juju", a word still used in a great

variety of ways. James Barbot, brother of the better-known writer, said that the people of Calabar called their idols "Jou-jou, being the nature of tutelar gods." The word juju is French, and means a little doll. But its application to African gods has been perpetuated mainly by English writers. One even finds a serious modern writer, P. A. Talbot in his series on Southern Nigeria, speaking of "minor deities or jujus", which he classes as inferior to the principal tribal deities. Even here not all would be plain sailing, and one often hears of an oath or ordeal as "making juju", and "juju or black magic". While I find in my morning paper in Nigeria an article entitled "The Church and the Juju Mask".

Confusion and injustice result from the continued use of this word also. Gods, however minor, are not toys. Many of them have no 'idols' anyway. This hoary word Juju can be dropped.

The Modern Picture

At the beginning of this chapter the objection was mentioned that African religion might not compare well with what are sometimes called the "higher religions", which have long histories, extensive sacred writings, and many temples and priests.

It is only on the second count that African religion suffers a handicap. The introduction of writing into the African tropics had to await the arrival of Europeans, and literary education did not begin before the nineteenth century. Consequently we have virtually no written texts to which men could refer back, no ancient prayers that throw light on earlier times, no old hymns or liturgies. But where there is no literature there is commonly a retentive memory, and many modern practices repeat the traditions of generations. A significant example of this is in the secret or ritual language to be found in some African cults. One finds that this ritual language, now not used for any other purpose, was the tongue of the original home of the cult. The language has been retained with the conservatism of religion, like that which retains Latin in the Roman liturgy and the Authorized Version in the English Church, and fragments of Greek and Hebrew in both.

The fact that there are no written texts does not mean that African religions have not a long history. The history of other faiths has often not been written until the advent of modern scholarship, and there are still large gaps in our knowledge of the early days even of Islam and Buddhism, not to mention the Celtic religions. In this respect the written religious history of the Hebrews, with which we are all familiar, is quite exceptional.

It has sometimes been assumed that because there was no written history or text therefore African religions are "primitive". This is to prejudge a very difficult question. Certainly Africans, like all other peoples, have a long history albeit unwritten. They are not "primitive" in the sense that they are somehow an older people than others, or in the sense that they have developed later and in some way show us the childhood of the race more clearly. It has merely too often been assumed that, because of the comparative isolation of tropical Africa till recent times, Africa must somehow show us how religion began or developed in its earlier stages; or that there was a stagnation and that African religion has been, as it were, fossilized until modern travellers came and unearthed it. This is a questionable assumption, because religion is a living thing.

Some modern writers have attempted to apply evolutionary concepts to African society and religion. But, however suitable these may be in biology, it does not follow that they can be applied strictly in the very different sphere of religion. In fact, modern theologians, after a period of deference to the evolutionists, are now beginning to stand on their own feet again and to question the validity of importing evolutionary concepts into religion at all. One need not follow the reaction too far, and refuse to recognize any development in religion. It is enough to assert that modern African religion need not be considered merely as "primitive religion".

For one thing, this consideration of African religion as essentially "primitive" leaves out of account altogether the possibility of revelations of God to Africans and inspiration by him. Such a question, theological no doubt and neglected by sociologists, is vital to the religious man of any race. Secondly, there are numerous writers on Africa who consider that Africans once worshipped one God alone, and that they have degenerated into polytheism. A similar view is held by those who believe in the diffusion of culture and religion from a common source, usually thought to be Egypt. Where modern peoples are below the level of the Egyptians that does not mean, it is contended, that they never attained such heights, but that they have lost their former achievements. So Africans may not be "primitive" but were, until recently, in a state of degeneration from a former high culture. One might say the same of the degeneration of some Europeans from Christianity to newspaper astrology.

These are theories: evolutionary, diffusionist, primitive monotheist, and the like. It is important to clear away the fog of such theories, in some degree, before going on to examine the facts. African religion has a history, which may be lost and may be ancient. It may have only dim reminiscences of prophets and reformers of the past, as has Hinduism, but such prophets are still appearing and continue the past traditions in new ways.

On the other hand, we must not glorify the unknown past so much, as some African nationalists tend to do, that we come to believe that African religion might "naturally" have developed of itself to the heights of Christianity. Infusion of new ideas from the outside has benefited all religions, and one undoubted factor in retarding African religion in the past has been the isolation of tropical Africa from the rest of the world. If nationalism closes the frontiers again that will be to its own impoverishment.

As for the innumerable temples and priests of other lands, they can well be paralleled in Africa. True there is no golden pagoda or mosque of Omar. African buildings were until recently mainly of perishable materials and there are few monuments of the past. Temples are small, though many of them are richly decorated with mouldings and paintings. Normally the African temple is only meant for the priest to enter, while the laity gather in the compound outside. In a hot country this is understandable, the Jerusalem temple was rather similar. There are many African priests and religious officials, mediums, diviners, doctors and their acolytes.

Finally, it is important now to treat of African religion separately from the religious beliefs of other parts of the world. In the past, books have been available dealing with some African beliefs along with those of Patagonia, Siberia, Australia and the North American Indians. Here there is great diversity and some beliefs which are prominent in America or Australia, for example totemism, are hardly to be found in Africa in any cultual form.

If one wished, in the past, to learn something of African beliefs one was obliged to hunt it out from the index of a work on Comparative Religion or Primitive Religion. Even then results would be very scanty, and three modern books which I consulted in this way referred to the Andamanese, the Arunta and the Aztecs, but not to the Ashanti or to Africa at all. The only way of gaining information has been to consult the special-ist monographs on various African tribes. These are expensive to buy, and are in very few public libraries. Even then they are restricted and refer in detail to some particular peoples.

With the increasing importance of Africa in the modern world, and the prominence in Africa of its religious life, it is necessary to provide a short account of the main religious beliefs and practices of many Africans. Such an account cannot pretend to completeness, since some tribes have not yet been the subject of research, but it is as full as possible under the cir-cumstances. It is based on the best modern scholarship, and it seeks to portray African religious beliefs as fairly and clearly as can be done.

CHAPTER II

A SPIRITUAL UNIVERSE

Animism and Psychic Force

IN 1871 Edward Tylor put forward the suggestion of "animism" or the theory of souls, as the fundamental concept of religion. Deriving animism from the Latin word *anima* for the soul, Tylor maintained that "belief in spiritual beings" or souls was the root of all religious faith. Animism could be taken as a "minimum definition of religion".

The idea of a soul is ancient, and Tylor thought it to be

derived from the breath, and also from the dreams in which dead people appear and so prompt the thought that their souls must be still alive. From thence men suppose that animals and even inanimate objects have souls. The sun and stars, winds, rivers, rocks, trees, all may have life and personality ascribed to them. So they may be talked to and invoked as intelligent beings.

This hypothesis has been criticized as too academic, and not fitting those peoples who believe in gods which have no apparent relationship to ghosts or spirits, but are "magnified non-natural men". Moreover it is questioned whether primitive men did clearly attribute souls and personalities to inanimate objects. Did he think of them rather vaguely as being endowed with life but no more? So in 1899 R. R. Marett coined the term "animatism", as a refinement of Tylor's animism. Animatism would represent the belief in impersonal spiritual power or a life-force pervading all things.

These are theories about the remote past. For, one must insist, all modern peoples have a long history and may hold beliefs very different from those of early man. Yet the word Animists is often applied to Africans, perhaps for lack of a better name and as superior to fetishers, pagans, or juju-worshippers. How far does animist or animatist correctly describe the African believer?

In recent years increasing stress has been laid upon the widespread African belief in psychic power. Father Tempels calls this "vital force", and Edwin Smith prefers the name "dynamism". The latter describes it as "The belief in, and the practices associated with the belief in hidden, mysterious, supersensible, pervading energy, powers, potencies, forces". The supreme value of the Bantu, says Tempels, is *"force, forceful living*, or *vital force"*. Many strange practices are done because people believe that "they serve to acquire *vigour* or *vital force, to live forcibly*, to reinforce life, or to assure its continuity in their descendants".[1]

In many parts of West Africa there is a word *nyama*, which European writers have sought to translate as energy, power, *force vitale, triebkraft*. From the western Sudan down to the Guinea Coast one finds variants of this word, sometimes

[1] *Lc. Philosophie Bantoue*, p. 27.

used as a title for God, sometimes of human or animal strength, or again as the mysterious force in medicines. *Nyama* is often conceived of as impersonal, unconscious energy, found in men, animals, gods, nature and things. *Nyama* is not the outward appearance, but the inner essence.

A medicine-man distinguishes between the tangible leaf or root, and the inward quality and power which is enshrined there. The medicine-man himself has *nyama*, as do outstanding men in special degree, such as woodcarvers, blacksmiths, hunters, orators, priests and chiefs. Witches are supposed to possess a similar power, purely psychically and independently of the use of any material means of harming their enemies; a look can kill. The psychic force may be used for conveying justice, vengeance, or hatred; it survives death and never perishes. Other words have similar meaning in different tribes: *baraka*, *kofi*, *ire*, *ashe*.

In East and Central Africa we find the concept of *bwanga*, which a Rhodesian writer calls "the power for healing or for destroying, for protecting or for hurting". This dynamism is found in the potency of charms and medicines, in rites of secret societies, in the preparations used by hunters and warriors, in ancestral ritual, and in the secret power of witches. A sinister feature of the belief is the conviction that sorcerers can tap this power for their nefarious purposes. As another writer says, it "is essentially the unseen power behind the concept of sorcery . . . the magical element of potency located in some material, the otherwise inexplicable".

The medicine-man is called by a cognate title, *nganga*, he is a manipulator of the power and he prays to God that it may come into the medicine that he is preparing. The doctor fills horns with his potent medicines and sells them as protections against all manner of evils. Priests may use them in their ritual and oracles. More than twenty Bantu languages use this term *bwanga*, and it is found on the other side of the Atlantic among the negroes of Carolina.

These beliefs are scarcely animistic, in the sense of attributing a personal soul to all beings and objects. They are more akin to the Melanesian belief in *mana*, an impersonal power regarded with great awe. The European thinks at once of electricity, for *nyama* and *bwanga* are like an energy or fluid, potent but non-moral. The Africans are more capable of abstract thought than is generally recognized, and they believe in a latent energy in things which is not visible in the outward appearance but can be seen in the effects produced by use.

Psychic Power and the gods

The psychic power appears in the world in different manifestations, which are explained as being in grades or a hierarchy. Thus there is not a wild confusion of forces, but explanations are given as to why some powers are more effective than others. Animals and plants have spiritual forces akin to those of men, but generally they are of lower grade than man's. Father Tempels says of the Bantu, "After the class of *human forces* come the other forces, those of animals, those of vegetables, and those of minerals. But in the midst of each of these classes is to be found a hierarchy according to the vital power, the rank, or the primogeniture . . . The respect for this rank of life, the care not to place oneself higher than one is or to keep in one's place, the necessity of not pushing up against superior forces as if they were equal, all this may furnish the key to the much disputed problem of 'totem' and 'taboo'."[1]

In this system of interacting forces come the spirits in which Africans believe. Some of them are personified as gods in animistic fashion, but they are still potent forces in human life. Professor Fortes says of the Tallensi of the Gold Coast that all "stand in awe of the Earth. We have learnt that they speak of it as a 'living thing', meaning by this that it intervenes mystically in human affairs in the same way as ancestral spirits do. When they talk of the Earth they mention its remorseless punishment of sacrilege."[2] Yet these people do not personify the Earth as a goddess. But other peoples do this, and the Ibo of Nigeria make images of Mother Earth with a child in her arms, like an Italian Madonna.

The spirits are, in the main, the ancestors and the forces of nature: the powers behind storm, rain, rivers, seas, lakes, wells, hills, rocks. They are not just the water or the rock,

[1]*La Philosophie Bantoue*, p. 42-44.
[2]*Dynamics of Clanship among the Tallensi*, p. 176.

for they are spiritual powers capable of manifesting themselves in many places. It is, as G. K. Chesterton insisted, not that men are so stupid as to worship the material sun, but the power and personality behind the sun. The power of the natural object may be met with at one of the shrines which are like its trysting-place with men.

In West Africa, in particular, men believe in great pantheons of gods which are as diverse as the gods of the Greeks or the Hindus. Many of these gods are the expression of the forces of nature, which men fear or try to propitiate. These gods generally have their own temples and priests, and their worshippers cannot justly be called Animists, but Polytheists, since they worship a variety of gods. The gods are not restricted to one spot, but many of them are ubiquitous and have numerous shrines; even if there is only one shrine the god is not imprisoned in it. It must never be forgotten that we have to do with a spiritual religion, however material it may appear at first sight.

All Africans believe in the ancestors, as ever-living and watchful. There is a great controversy as to whether African practices may be called "ancestor-worship", and as such properly religious, or whether Africans revere their dead fathers as they respect a living chief. But no one denies that the ancestors are regarded as having powers which are useful to men, and the dilemma concerning worship may be resolved by the philosophy of forces. The ancestors were human, but they have acquired additional powers and men seek to obtain their blessing or avert their anger by due offerings.

Above all is the Supreme Being. There is a much more general belief in him than has been thought in the past. Often he is considered to be so remote that men do not pray to him regularly. But in time of great distress many Africans turn to God in desperation. He is the final resort, the last court of appeal, and he may be approached directly without intermediary. The power of God is supreme; all flows from him and inheres in him. Godlings and ancestors are intermediaries; prayers and offerings made to them may be passed on to the source of all.

The relationship between these spiritual powers has been

aptly represented by a triangle. At the apex is the sky, which symbolizes the Supreme Power from whom all life flows and to whom all returns. The base is the earth, sometimes personified as a goddess, but always important to man as the producer of his food and the burying-place of his dead. On the earth lives man, and his chiefs and kings are rungs in the ladder between himself and God. On one side of the triangle are the ancestors, rising up in the hierarchy by their increased powers. Dead kings and chiefs are their leaders and potent to help or harm. On the other side of the triangle are the gods, or natural forces, which must be propitiated lest they become angry at neglect and cause the seasons to fail.

"Man beneath the sky" lives on the land, not in a void but as a sovereign vital force. He has no doubt that he was made to have dominion "over every living thing that moveth upon the earth". It is his duty to "be fruitful, and multiply, and replenish the earth, and subdue it". On the other hand he knows that he is not able to do these things by himself, and he seeks the help of every available power, spirits and gods "that share this earth with man as with their friend".

Religion and Magic

Parallel to the debate about the relationship of ancestor-worship and religion, is that over the connexion of magic with religion.

Sir James Frazer used to contend that magic was an elementary form of science, since it proceeded on the belief that cause produces effect. Yet he called it a bastard science, for it misapplied the principles of causation and similarity. He further maintained that magic was older than religion; that there was an age of magic when men tried to control nature by sheer force of spells and enchantments, but when they found these to fail they looked for higher powers and accepted the belief in gods and personal powers beyond man on whom he depends for help.

All this is speculative. There is little evidence for the primary occurrence of magic. In addition, Frazer failed to take into account the spiritual character of magic, its constant belief in the power of dynamism behind things, in which it differs widely from modern science. In Africa, at least, it cannot now be held (as some writers on comparative religion state) that magic is confined to mechanical actions and does not refer to supernatural powers. The efficacy of magical practices does not merely reside in things done or said, but in the employment of a supernatural agency, a psychic power.

Dr. Edwin Smith, in a lecture on *African Symbolism*, suggests that magic is another of these words that have become archaic and misleading, and that it "might now be given a decent burial and that we should rather speak of various levels or stages or phases of religion". To replace the word magic this writer would use the term dynamism.

What have been called magical acts are innumerable in African life, and they depend upon the belief in the utilization of invisible powers. The occult power is believed to dwell in the countless charms which people wear on their bodies, in the medicines made by a doctor, and in the ritual actions of a hunter or warrior. The symbols that men use, masks, colours, numbers, names, metaphors, all link up with the energy in the desired object; they are not dead symbols.

Magic, or dynamism, is a part of the belief in a spiritual world which is found all over Africa. It cannot be said that Africans are simply animists, believing in personal spirits and polytheistic pantheons. Nor are they merely animatists, thinking of unco-ordinated energies. A few writers would even call them monotheists, since all powers are subject to the Supreme Being. But this again would over-simplify the picture.

The fact is that we find mixed types of religious belief, in which different phases are found side by side: dynamism, spiritism and theism. The spiritual powers are ranked in hierarchies and approached according to need. Magical charms are made for teething troubles, ancestors are consulted over land disputes, sky gods are prayed to for rain, above all is the great Creator. All these powers are important, and in turn they may help man in his incessant fight against disease, drought or witchcraft.

Religion and Society

This chapter deals with psychic powers and the spiritual world, but it should be clear that there is no sharp dividing-line between sacred and secular such as we profess to have in Europe. Material and spiritual are intertwined, the former as a vehicle of the latter. This life and the next are scarcely divided by "the narrow stream of death". Those who have crossed to that further shore are with us still, in dreams, in offerings, in rites performed and oracles consulted. Indeed they are nearer than before, and as being invisible one cannot tell when they are around.

Religion is not just the province of one particular class, though there are specialists in ritual. Nor is it only for those who feel piously inclined, though there are differences of temperament. But religion enters into the life of every individual, and there are certain transitional rites through which everybody has to pass in the older societies.

The whole organization of society is maintained by the spiritual forces which pervade it. This is brought out clearly in an important study of *African Political Systems*. The authors stress the importance of religious symbols, rites, dogmas, sacred places and persons in unifying African society and giving it cohesion and persistence. These sacred symbols endow the social system "with mystical values which evoke acceptance of the social order that goes far beyond the obedience exacted by the secular sanction of force. The social system is, as it were, removed to a mystical plane, where it figures as a system of social values beyond criticism or revision".[1]

The religious beliefs enshrine the attitude of men to their daily needs, and the way in which their satisfaction is safeguarded. "The African sees these ritual observances as the supreme safeguard of the basic needs of his existence and of the basic relations that make up his social order—land, cattle, rain, bodily health, the family, the clan, the state. The mystical values reflect the general import of the basic elements of existence."

Moreover religion provides the sanctions that society cannot fully supply of itself, its "moral and legal norms which

[1] By M. Fortes and E. Evans-Pritchard, p. 16 ff.

could not be kept in being as a body, by secular sanctions. Periodical ceremonies are necessary to affirm and consolidate these values because, in the ordinary course of events, people are pre-occupied with sectional and private interests and are apt to lose sight of the common interest and of their political interdependence."

European students of African society may have their own private doubts as to the validity of the orthodox spiritual approach to life. No one can deny that the spiritual is fundamental to African life. The European may be puzzled by the supernatural aspects of African society and organization, but he cannot evade its presence and importance to the whole of society.

The mystical element in social life is often crystallized in the person of the king or chief. The chief is not merely a secular ruler, who can be replaced by a foreign district officer, but he is hedged by "a divinity" of his own. The chief may be a bad man, and can be removed from office by the proper officials, but the office of kingship remains unaffected by such change and it persists as the focus of mystical values.

If an illegitimate nominee is put forward for succession to a chieftaincy by a European government, then the people may easily revolt. And they will do so on mystical grounds. They will say, "It is not possible for such a one to be chief. Nothing will grow any more on our soil, the women will bear no more children, the skies will not send rain, and all will be smitten with sterility". To the outsider this seems illogical. But to the African it is the direct consequence of disturbing the very foundations of order. "Unnatural deeds do breed unnatural troubles".

This world is a spiritual arena, in which is seen the interplay of psychic forces. This is the African belief, and while its application may not always appear correct, the religious man of any race will agree with the principle. The agnostic sociologist and psychologist may seek to explain away this belief and its rites as projections and symbols, social constructs which have subjective and not objective value. In the words of Edwin Smith, "In these matters I prefer to stand with the Africans".

THE PANTHEONS

CHAPTER III

THE SUPREME BEING

God and the Ancestors

IN various chapters of this book we shall have to consider the interaction of religion and social life. There have been writers on African society who have maintained that belief in a Supreme God is due to the influence of a hierarchical society, and that God is nothing more than a glorified chief or ancestor. This is a very ancient notion. The Greek philosopher Euhemeros of Macedonia (320–260 B.C.) said that the gods were departed chiefs and warriors, who had been venerated before their death and deified afterwards. From this he deduced that all the gods came from human ancestors, and that the myths concerning them enshrined memories of historical events. In the nineteenth century of our era Herbert Spencer, a voluminous but sometimes inexact writer, upheld a similar opinion. "Using the phrase ancestor-worship", he said, "in its broadest sense as comprehending all worship of the dead, be they of the same blood or not, we reach the conclusion that ancestor-worship is the root of every religion".

In Africa a Gold Coast writer, J. B. Danquah, has declared that the Supreme God of the Akan is a deified ancestor: "Akan knowedge of God teaches that he is the Great Ancestor." God, according to this writer, is the primordial ancestor of the tribe, "As such ancestor he deserves to be worshipped, and is worshipped in the visible head, the good chief of the community". Other writers on the Akan, however, deny this assertion and say that there is no trace of the identification of God with the first father of the tribe.

Sir James Frazer wrote a book, entitled *The Worship of Nature*, dealing largely with African beliefs in a Supreme God. He came to the conclusion that belief in God in Africa, so far from originating in ancestor-worship, was a reflection of the worship of nature. Frazer began his book with the words,

"The mind of man refuses to acquiesce in the phenomena of sense," and hence man seeks for something more abiding than the sensible world and conceives the idea of spiritual beings".

Other writers, particularly Father Schmidt and certain missionaries, believe that Africans originally had a belief in one God, divinely inspired, and that they fell from this belief into the polytheism in which we find them today. A missionary in Nigeria, Farrow, thought that the belief these people have in a Supreme God above many secondary gods "is plainly the remnant of an ancient monotheism".

One priest even traces a supposed African monotheism back to the Jews, who he thinks were dispersed in Africa. Then there is a popular theory that African religion derives from Egypt. Dr. Lucas maintains that almost the whole of the West African gods can be traced back to Egypt.

These arguments are too complex to be resolved here, and the whole question of religious origins is very involved. The essential historical evidence is lacking. Those who hold that the idea of one God over all reflects a monarchical society must reckon with the fact that peoples of very different social organization have a belief in one God; the monarchical Ashanti believed in a great God and worshipped him, the equally monarchical Yoruba believed in him but had no organized worship, while the much less centralized and more individualistic Ibo and Kikuyu believed in God but the latter had regular worship while the former had not.

For our purpose it suffices to show that there are variant theories of the origin of the belief in God in Africa, none is conclusive, and we are concerned with practice rather than theory. The fact is that most African peoples have clear beliefs in a Supreme God, and others while less clear at least have some spiritual beliefs. The day has gone when one can write, as did a seventeenth-century traveller in South Africa, "No one, however thoroughly he has inquired, has ever been able to find among all the Kafirs, or Hottentots, or Beach-rangers any trace of religion, or any show of honour to God or the Devil". Today so much more is known of the languages and social organization of these people that, even when they have adopted

Christianity, their ancient beliefs are often discoverable. To these beliefs we now proceed.

Belief in a Supreme Creator

The Mende people of Sierra Leone believe in a creator God called Ngewo. He existed from the beginning and is the author of all life, of the visible world and men and the invisible spirits. God filled the universe with an immaterial power which is seen in striking ways, such as in lightning and waterfalls, and which also appear at times in outstanding men. All power comes from God, who is omnipotent but not immanent. His name is frequently on men's lips, in salutations, blessings and prayers: "God give you long life," "God take care of you." "God is judge," and similar words and proverbs indicate the finality and inevitability of God's actions and judgements. Their neighbours, the Kono people, speak of God as the omnipresent and eternal, who lives through all the generations of man, although he is far away in the sky. Men can appeal to God for justice and he rewards evil-doers with lightning, barrenness or inexplicable death.

One of the clearest and best known examples of belief in God is to be found among the Ashanti of the Gold Coast. They call God 'Nyame, and this name in one form or another (Nyam, Nyonmo, Nyama) is found widely distributed in West Africa. It is probably different from another God-name (Nzambi, Nyambe) found in Central and South Africa, from the Cameroons to Bechuanaland.

Recent writers on the Ashanti have spoken of 'Nyame as female, the great Mother, who gives life to all and is symbolized by the moon. Under another aspect the sun appears as a personification of the supreme God. There is probably a duality of sex in this conception, the famous Dr. Aggrey spoke as a Christian of Father-Mother God. Myths tell that God created three realms in the universe: heaven, earth and the underworld. 'Nyame rules over the sky, a goddess of procreation over the earth, and old Mother Earth over the underworld, that is over the dead who "lie buried in her pocket".

The Gã of the Gold Coast use a similar name, Nyonmo, for God. He is essentially a god of rain and so is supreme over other gods in this land where rain is so important. The name Nyonmo may be translated Nature, for "Nyonmo's death" means a natural one, not a death due to foul play. The answer given to inscrutable problems is that it is God or Nature.

An apparent identification of God with the sun has been thought to exist among peoples in the north of the Gold Coast and Nigeria. However, although they use a word for the Supreme Being which means "the sun", they are not sun-worshippers whatever their ancestors may have been. The sun and God are frequently distinguished in speech by suffixes, and God means to them the whole firmament, they say: "the sun falls in the evening, but he (God) is always there". The sun may be called the son of God and the earth his wife. Rivers get their powers from him, and rich men derive from him their wealth. Soothsayers obtain their supernatural powers from God, and even the dead rise up to request of him increase of children and fertility of crops. Men may stretch out their hands to the rising sun in the morning and pray for blessing, but other tribes do this who have different ideas of the Supreme Being.

In Nigeria the Yoruba people call God Olorun, which has the clear meaning of "owner of the sky". He is believed in by everybody as the creator of all things, the almighty and all-knowing, the giver of life and breath, and the final judge of all men. Although he is a great and distant God yet his name is daily heard in salutations, blessings, proverbs and riddles. Because of his greatness and the obvious derivation of his name, it has been suggested that this idea of God was borrowed from Muslims or Christians, but there is no evidence for this The new religions adopt and enrich the name of God, but do not introduce it as something new. Similar ideas are held by the Ibo of Nigeria.

Among the Congo tribes the Ngombe believe in a supreme spirit called Akongo (nothing to do with the word Congo, the vowels and tones are different). This is the chief God of the tribe and their ancestors, and they say that all peoples have a name for him. They deny that God was ever a man, he is a spirit even if he has human features. Akongo is the creator of the universe, the moulder of men like a potter. He is called Beginner, and Unending, Almighty and Inexplicable. He is closely related to each individual, as a guardian spirit, giving good fortune or bad. He is easily approached, though he has no temples or idols.[1]

Crossing over to East Africa we find that the Baganda people of Uganda have become so widely Christianized that it is difficult to disentangle their old beliefs from the new associations which have been brought to them. Katonda is the name used for God and adopted by Christians. He is central to Baganda belief, but other sources of power are consulted at need, often a prophet or the dead. God is creator, protector and helper; his name is used in blessings and proverbs. He creates (*kutonda*) children, and moulds them in a woman's body. It is said that God joins the water and blood from man and woman, and set them in a mould as if it were clay.

The Kikuyu of Kenya believe in a Supreme God called Murungu. He is believed to live on four sacred mountains, though he is also all-pervading and invisible. He is called "Possessor of Whiteness", perhaps because of his association with the sky. One finds in many parts of Africa this connexion of the Supreme God and his priests with whiteness. God is the creator of all things. He shows his power in sun, moon and stars, in storm and rain, and in the rainbow. Prayers were made to him by all men at night and in the morning as the sun was rising, though it was not sun-worship.

The name Murungu or Mulungu is found among some twenty-five tribes of East Africa. In Nyasaland he is the creator, the God of storms and rain, and his voice is heard in the thunder. He is everywhere, can do all things, and is formless. His power pervades all things, and some attribute the power of witches to him.

A favourite East African name for God is Leza. This is used in Rhodesia, Tanganyika and the upper Congo. The name may come from a verb meaning "to cherish", as a mother does her child or a chief his people. With the Tonga this name means the First Cause, creator of all, heat and cold, famine and

---

[1]Not a great deal is yet available on the pygmies of the Congo. But the researches of Schebesta have shown that, contrary to what used to be supposed, the pygmies have positive religious beliefs in a Creator God and in spiritual beings.

disease. "God falls," "God blows," are said of rain and wind. When exceptional harvests or unexpected deliverances occur men say "God is our Father". In Rhodesia the Ba-ila speak of Leza as the Moulder or Constructor. He created all things and established the customs of the tribe. He is everlasting, everywhere, the one from whom all comes, and the owner of all. He gives the elements: "Leza rains," "Leza blows". The lightning is his bow, and the thunder is Leza beating his rugs.

The Basuto called the Supreme Being Molimo: Light, Protector and Father. It is difficult to say what the older ideas were as these people have been influenced by Christianity. The older Basuto are all said to have known a prayer which requested the lesser gods to pray to the God of old for men. If sudden death came from lightning men would say, "God has killed him". The Bechuana used a similar name (Morimo) for God. David Livingstone noted that the use of this name spread rapidly among the Bechuana and the older men said that their fathers spoke of God in the same way. It seems that the mention of the name of the Creator has been a great taboo, "the mere mention of which in the ears of the people would cause death to the profane one". This taboo, similar to the Jewish taboo on the use of the name Jehovah, was one reason why early travellers thought that these people had no belief in God.

There has been considerable controversy whether the Zulu word Unkulunkulu, commonly translated God, is properly applied to the Supreme Being, or whether there is confusion with an aboriginal man. Perhaps before the coming of Christianity these two ideas existed and were confused later. The word means "great, great one", or "old, old one", and this Ancient of days is said to have created all things, and to be the ancestor of men whose society he ordered. But the Zulu also had another name, "Lord of heaven", or "chief in the sky", which may not have been a proper name, perhaps because his name was taboo, but which had praise names attached to it referring especially to his action in storms.

Finally, there are some people who have only a very vague idea of God. The Lovedu of northern Transvaal have a tradition concerning the Creator of the world and men. It is said

that he left footprints on rocks when they were soft, but today
he is otiose and men seem not to know what became of him and
give him no thought. The Swazi likewise have a vague belief in a
First Being, who is like a great ancestor. He made the earth and
men, and eventually sent death to men. But the ancestors
came between him and mankind, and he has become remote,
not mentioned in prayer nor intervening in morals. He used
sometimes to send a one-legged messenger from the sky, to
appear to women and children, and this was the prelude to
fever and so men propitiated him with goats and cattle, and
even made a pretence of offering their children to him.

The Worship of God

The above may read like a catalogue of tribes, although
only some of the more important have been mentioned.
But it is necessary to give an outline of belief in God, in view
of the wild assertions sometimes made about African belief or
lack of belief in God. Those who need more detail may be
referred to *African Ideas of God* or *The Worship of Nature*.

The question as to how far God is worshipped is important.
One of the clearest examples of regular worship in West Africa
is among the Dogon of the French Sudan. Here there are group
altars for God (Amma) which are communal property and the
chief is usually the officiant. There are also special people
who give personal service to God and become his priests.
Normally such persons are possessed by a strange force, and on
the advice of a diviner they consecrate themselves to the service
of God. A woman may find a sacred object and build an altar
to God there or at her home, with earth taken from the spot
where she found the object; there she will sacrifice. A priest
(called "companion of Amma") offers regular sacrifices, after
he has been consecrated with special rites. Priests and priestesses
officiate at annual ceremonies, they observe taboos of some
foods, and are believed to be endowed with second sight that
enables them to see the souls that are going to die.

Early travellers said that the Ashanti of the Gold Coast
did not worship God. But there are some temples for him,
not in public but in old palaces. These temples are decorated
with symbols of the heavens, and are served by priests who wear

gold and silver ornaments representing moons. But in addition to this every family compound has a "God's tree", a forked branch which holds a basin or pot containing water and a "God's axe", an old stone implement believed to have come down from heaven during a thunder-storm. In these pots or on the roofs of their huts people place daily offerings for the great God of the sky. Similarly in the northern Gold Coast sacrifices are made to God and offered at shrines that are clay moulds. A diviner holds up a fowl to show it to God and says, "Sky-God descend and receive your guinea-fowl that you have demanded".

The Kikuyu of Kenya worship the great God at shrines that are sacred fir-trees or groves. Here God was believed to come and no tree might be cut or animal allowed to damage it. The grove was a sanctuary for fugitives. Sacrifices were made here of rams without blemish. Part of the meat was left for God at the foot of a tree, and the rest was eaten by the worshippers as a communion sacrifice. God was worshipped at special times of need, in drought and epidemics, and also in gratitude for good harvests. He was approached also at the turning-points in individual life, at birth, initiation, marriage and death of every Kikuyu.

But in many parts of Africa one finds the strange phenomenon that God is believed in yet is thought of as so great and remote that he is offered no regular worship. The Mende of Sierra Leone believe that after the creation God retired into the heavens and has little to do with the world now. God can, however, be approached through intermediaries. Indeed, part of this concept of a distant God, with intervening spirits, is like that of a mighty chief who is inaccessible on most occasions but is approached in time of special need. Normally men pray to the lesser gods and ancestors. Yet in times of distress men may pray directly to God, without any intermediary. These unmediated prayers are spontaneous and short.

Most Nigerian peoples think the same. The Ibo rarely sacrifices to God (Chuku), but a family-head may put some kola nuts on the ground in the early morning and ask God to watch over him and his children. Other gifts may be made occasionally; travellers beginning a journey, or traders commencing some enterprise will invoke God's blessing. Even if sacrifice to God is rare yet all offerings to lesser gods are regarded as ultimately destined to God; the sacrificer will say, "Chuku eat kola, Ala eat kola, ancestors eat kola." Formerly slaves might be given to God through the mediation of some lesser being.

Leza has no ceremonies in Rhodesia, he is too far away and fearful. The lesser divinities act as intermediaries, and may be asked to pray to God for men. In time of special need one may pray to God, when sickness is incurable and other gods fail, then God is called upon for "his ears are long".

The Ovambo of South-West Africa pray to Kalunga for help in need and ask his blessing of children, they make sacrifice in time of drought, but more frequently pray to the spirit of the storm and to the ancestors. Similarly the Hottentots made animal sacrifices to God in time of need, and annual prayer was made by the community asking for rain and good harvests.

The general picture in Africa is that regular communal prayers to God are rare. Temples and priests are few, and only found among certain tribes, such as Dogon, Ashanti and Kikuyu. But individual prayer is widely practised, especially in time of exceptional necessity. God is the resort of the desperate, when all else has failed. Then, despite his greatness and distance, he can be appealed to directly, without special formulas or intervening priests or godlings.

Names of God

The names given to God indicate what men think about his character and attributes. A selection is given here from those collected in *African Ideas of God*, to which reference may be made for fuller details and particulars of the tribes which have their own peculiar ideas.

God as Creator is one of the commonest aspects that men have understood, so we get names such as: Creator, Moulder, Creator of souls, Giver of breath, God of destinies.

God in nature is expressed in titles such as: Giver of rain, One who brings round seasons, Giver of sunshine, The great bow in the heavens, He who thunders from far-off, The fire-lighter.

The omnipotence and omniscience of God are indicated by the names: He who gives and rots, The ancient of days, The limitless, The One from the first, The irresistible, The wise one, He who bends down even majesties, He who roars so that all nations are struck with terror, He who is of himself, The One you meet everywhere.

Many titles express the providence of God: Father of little babies, Father of the placenta, The great Mother, Father-mother God, the kindly-disposed, Greatest of friends, Master of the forest, The providence who watches over all like the sun, God full of pity, God of comfort, The one on whom men lean and do not fall.

Finally there are those names which are mysterious, enigmatic, or apparently bizarre: The great pool contemporary of everything, The immense ocean whose circular headdress is the horizon, He who is beyond all thanks, The one who clears the forest, The high up one, The inexplicable, He who was found, The angry one, The greatness of the bow, The great spider.

Myths about God

Africans love stories, and there are many myths about gods and spirits. A German scholar, Baumann, analysed some 2,500 African myths for their theology and cosmology. Here we can only indicate a few types which shed light upon the belief in the nature of God.

Firstly there is a widespread story to explain how it is that God and the sky are so far away. This may link with ancient and classical tales of a past Golden Age when men walked with God, some writers call these Paradise myths. Often in African story a woman is blamed for having brought the idyllic state to an end. The Margi of Nigeria say that in the past the sky could be touched and there was no need to work, God filled men's calabashes without them working; but a woman put out a dirty calabash and infected the finger of one of the sky children, and God retired in anger to his present distance. Elsewhere they say that a woman annoyed God by hitting the sky with her pounding-stick, or women tore pieces of the sky to put in the soup and God went off to a distance.

The Ngombe of the Congo say that men used to live in the sky, but one woman became such a nuisance that God lowered her down from heaven in a basket with enough seed for herself and her children. In Urundi it is thought that God used to live with men and created their children. One day he made a crippled baby and the parents were so angry that they took a knife to kill God, and so he retired. The Ba-ila of Rhodesia simply said that Leza is not so young as he used to be or so near. He has got old, and just as old men dribble tears so the rain is his dribbling. He is not so accessible to prayers as he used to be.

Rather like the Garden of Eden story is that of the Mende, who say that God once lived in a cave and invited the animals to come in pairs but forbade them to touch his food. One day the cow smelt the sweet-smelling food and ate some, and at once God seized the animal and threw it out of the cave. The monkey and all the animals eventually sinned and suffered the same fate, including man. Now all the animals wander about looking for that delicious food, and God watches them from above. Men did not pray at first, until God gave them a mountain whose voice they could hear. The Dogon of the Sudan also say that God originally had no altars, but he came in the guise of a beggar asking for drink, and the good man who received him was shown how to make an altar.

Next is the very common myth of the origin of death. In this the chief roles are played by animals: a dog, a chameleon or a sheep. The general drift of the story is that God told men they would not die, or that they would live again. He sent the message by a dog or a chameleon, but this animal tarried on the way and another animal, a lizard, toad or hare, arrived first and told men that they would die, and so they buried their corpses and they could not be raised up again. One version says that God was angry and smote the hare with his cleft lip; another that men are angry with the chameleon and always chase it away and the reptile changes its colour. Other versions put the story the other way round, that men send to God and the slow messenger arrives first and God refuses to change his decree for the second messenger. What was behind Aesop's fable of the hare and the tortoise?

Sometimes the snake enters in. The Kono of Sierra Leone say that God sent men new skins in a package; the dog who was taking the parcel delayed and it was stolen by the snake who now knows how to change his skin and does not die unless he is killed. That the snake is immortal is a common belief; at times the snake is regarded as a reincarnation of the ancestors. There may be a link here with the snake in Eden, and there is perhaps one also in the Ashanti story that the first man and woman had no knowledge of conception and hence no children. The python taught them to procreate by making couples stand facing each other and spraying their bellies with water, then telling them to go home and sleep together. Women conceived and bore children, and the python is still sacred to some Ashanti clans.

The Kono say that at the beginning of the world the night was not dark and men could see clearly. But God one day gave the bat a hamper containing darkness to take up to the moon, and said he would come later on to say what should be done with it. Like the dog and chameleon in other stories, the bat delayed to eat food on the way and other animals peeped in the hamper. The darkness immediately came out and covered the earth at night, till the sun came to chase it away. Ever since then the bat flies about at night trying to get hold of the darkness to carry it up to the moon.

Conclusion

The belief in, prayers to, names of and myths about God show clearly that nearly all Africans, "untutored" though some may be, do conceive of God. For most of them God was the creator of all things, but he has withdrawn to that remoteness which is part of his greatness. Like the most mighty of kings he is only rarely approached, and the intervening gods and ancestors receive much more attention from the common man. In time of great need, however, when all else has failed, God can be resorted to directly without priest or temple. Some of this belief may reflect the organization of society, with its chiefs and petty rulers, but the direct appeal to God savours more of a democracy which many peoples have not known.

The old evolutionary theory, which some writers have applied to Africa in the hope that it might show the early stages of religion, in animism or animatism, finds in the belief in God no very strong support. It is just as arguable that there was an ancient monotheistic belief from which men fell away. Neither theory is provable as things are. And now come Christianity and Islam into tropical Africa, with their missionary fervour and clear theology, and the old God comes forth from his seclusion, with new attributes, but doubtless bringing some of his old features into the new religions.

CHAPTER IV

NATURE GODS

IF one were to speak of African religions, in the plural, one main distinction would be between those peoples who worship nature gods and those who do not. Over the greater part of pagan Africa one passes almost direct from belief in a Supreme Being to faith in ancestral spirits. Some of the most advanced and sophisticated peoples, however, interpose natural and hero gods between God and the ancestors.

Roughly it may be said that the peoples of Central and Southern Africa have not developed belief in nature gods, whereas many of the leading peoples of West Africa have large pantheons of gods. But some of the Sierra Leone tribes, in the far west, regard the ancestors as all-important and have only vague beliefs in other spirits.

"Nature spirits and hero gods have no place in the scheme of things" believed in by the Lovedu of the Transvaal, we are told. But most of the Bantu believe in natural and local spirits, which may be those of the departed, or "dissociated spirits, often vague and shadowy in character, but none the less terrifying and dangerous to the traveller". There are spirits of mountains and forests, of pools and streams, of trees and other local objects.

There are numerous animal spirits and sacred snakes which may assist in rain-making. The Zulu talk of a female spirit Inkosazana who helps the corn to grow, and for whom maidens perform springtime rites in the fields.

The Mende of Sierra Leone believe in nature spirits or genii which are associated with rivers and forests. The genie may appear in human form and white colour, and seek to entrap the unwary traveller. As a water sprite she may be a siren with beautiful hair, like the Lorelei, and equally dangerous to those whom she fascinates. As forest sprite a genie may appear as an old white man with a white beard, seeking to befog travellers with his questions and make them lose their way in the bush. Although there is no earth cult here, yet the Supreme God is sometimes spoken of as having a partner here below: "O God, you and your wife the earth."

It is possible that writers in some parts of Africa have not paid sufficient attention to the manifestations of polytheism. The ancestral cult has appeared all-important. The nature spirits have little apparent worship paid to them. Yet even where there is no temple or general worship of the spirit of the earth or of the storm, men may still hold them in great awe, and believe that their power is great.

It is in West Africa, however, that we find fully-developed polytheism. Here are pantheons of nature gods, with their temples and priests, like the polytheisms of Egypt, Greece and India. These will be considered in the rest of this chapter.

Sun, Moon and Sky
It might be expected that cults of the sun and moon would play a large part in the life of African peoples, since such cults were of great importance in ancient Egyptian religion. But in fact such worship is rare even in the pantheons of West Africa. Perhaps the sun is too oppressive in West Africa, and not the object of such longing expectation as in northern latitudes where its return from the south in the spring was anxiously awaited. Similarly the moon is important to nomads and desert dwellers, but less to the inhabitants of the tropical forest. But if actual worship is scanty, the sun does figure in the religion of some peoples.

Nyankopon, the truly great Nyame (God) is said to be personified by the sun to the Ashanti of the Gold Coast. He is symbolized by the four-limbed cross, indicating the four points of the compass, and also he is represented by golden disks, scarabs and birds. The king may be thought of as an impersonation of the sun, and hence the dynamic centre of the state as the sun is of the sky, and the king's golden ornaments are of the colour of the eternal fire of the sun. Many golden objects, stools, drums, horns, lutes, axes, are of symbolical significance.[1]

The Ewe of Dahomey associate one of the divine pair (Mawu-Lisa) with the sun. In a well-known carving Lisa has the sun's disk in his mouth, while Mawu carries a crescent moon.

Some of the Ibo of Nigeria have shrines of the sun, who is a child of the Supreme God. The symbol of the god is a branch of a tree planted outside a dwelling-hut, and sometimes a pottery dish in front of it is said to represent the sun's disk.

The moon may be called upon in individual rites. The Queen Mother of Ashanti is said to be regarded as the daughter of the moon, the female aspect of the Supreme Being. Silver is her colour; she wears silver adornments, and at death the openings of her body are filled with silver dust. The importance of the queen mother in affairs of state, overlooked by early writers, is recognized now as decisive.

Some of the tribes of Dahomey have an official "moon-glorifier", whose task is to assist in the coming-out ceremonies of new-born children and their mothers. This man sounds a little horn and tells the mother to suckle her child when the new moon appears. Others get an aunt to lift the baby up to the moon saying, "Look at the moon, little one; we bless you at the coming of the new moon. When you see the moon, you see riches, prosperity and long life". Yoruba mothers in Nigeria bring their children out of the hut a week after birth and throw water on the roof which is allowed to fall on the baby. The same is done to Gã children in the Gold Coast who are laid naked on the ground while water falls on them from the roof; so they are introduced to rain and to the earth. Some northern tribes hold

[1]This interpretation is that of Eva Meyerowitz in *The Sacred State of the Akan*, chapters III-IV.

a baby up to the rising sun, three times for a boy and four times
for a girl.

When a Nigerian Ibo sees the new moon he says, holding up
his hands, "New moon, protect me as the last moon protected
me". He may ask the new moon to bring him better luck this
month. Other tribes salute the new moon, and even Muslims
may pour libations of milk on graves at the new moon's appearing.

Comparable vagueness is found regarding the sky, which
may be thought of as a son of God but have no proper cult.
The sky is the abode of God but, despite language in which they
seem to be identical, and myths of God removing to the present
distance of the sky, God is normally thought of as above and
beyond the sky. We may speak of sky-gods, such as the Supreme
Being or the gods of storms, but these are not identical with the
firmament of heaven. "The sun falls in the evening time, but
God is always there", say people in the northern Gold Coast,
and a similar remark might be made about the sky. The Lobi
of this region believe in a God-atmosphere, but he has no cult
except when he is revered under the forms of lightning and
thunderbolt. The circle of heaven may fertilize the earth as a
man his wife, but the rain and the storm receive attention rather
than the vault above.

Storm Gods

Gods of the storm are divinities in full right in many parts
of West Africa. They have temples, priests and regular worship.

The Yoruba and Ibo of Nigeria, and the Ewe of Dahomey
and Togo, pay such attention to storm, lightning, thunder and
thunderbolt, that although, doubtless, they might be included
with the sky gods, yet they are better regarded as forming a
Storm Pantheon in its own right. In many places the storm gods
have the greatest and most powerful temples, and their priests
are recognized as leaders before most others. This is only to
be expected, in this land of violent storms and torrential
rain.

Most Ibo villages have a shrine of the god of lightning,
whose symbols are a tree with two pots in front. Annual
rites are performed here, before the yam harvest; chickens are

sacrificed which are shared among worshippers and the village chief.

The Yoruba god Shango, god of lightning and thunder, is worshipped along with his wives, who are notable rivers, and with the rainbow and thunderclap which are his attendants. He is called "Fighter with Stone", or "The Stone-Thrower". In his temples are to be seen stones that are probably ancient implements, but they are believed by the worshippers to be thunderbolts come down from heaven. One of these is said to fall whenever a house is struck by lightning, and the priests make a great ado looking for these stones. Shango is not only a storm god, but also a deified hero, believed to have been the fourth king of Oyo, the ancient Yoruba capital. He is thought to have been able to call down fire from heaven but with disastrous results; the fire destroyed his own family and in remorse he went and hanged himself. Priests still claim to be able to draw down the lightning or thunderbolt, but say that it is risky for they themselves to practise it.

The storm god of the Ewe is borrowed from the Yoruba; "thunder stones"; double-headed axes, and symbolical rams are found in both cults. In Ashanti the thunder is assimilated to the Supreme God who has "thunder stones" in his small altars, the rainbow as his arch and forked sticks as his sacred trees.

Mother Earth

The earth, as mother of plants, animals and men, is of great importance to many West African peoples, as it was to ancient Europeans under the names of Demeter and Ceres, the earth mother.

In a number of places the earth is revered but has no regular cultus. In the north of the Gold Coast the Tallensi speak of the earth as "a living thing". They call certain taboo animals "the people of the earth". The earth is a mystical power of which everybody stands in awe, because of its prohibitions and its punishments. The earth forbids bloodshed and so is a sanction of solidarity for the community. There are earth shrines, the places of localized worship for social groups. Yet the earth does not seem to be clearly personified as a goddess, with images such as are to be seen in Nigeria. A similar attitude to the earth as that of the Tallensi is found in many parts of the western Sudan.

The Ashanti believe that the earth is animated by a female principle whose sacred day is Thursday, and so the spirit is called "Thursday Earth." Yet the earth has no priests and is not consulted by divination in time of sickness as are other gods. The Ashanti says, "The earth is not a goddess, she does not divine." But the earth is of great importance in life, work is forbidden on the land on Thursdays lest she be disturbed, and this has given rise to conflict with the introduction of the Christian Sunday rest. Before hoeing the land farmers propitiate the earth with offerings of fowls and yams, and at harvest they return thanks to the earth with a libation or a sacrifice. Libations are also made when graves are dug, for it is the earth that receives the dead "into her pocket". Especially is the earth concerned with the disposal of land which is owned by the ancestors.

The drummers address the earth in the ancestral ceremonies held every three weeks:

> "Earth, while I am yet alive,
>   It is upon you that I put my trust,
> Earth who receives my body . . .
> We are addressing you,
> And you will understand."[1]

At a grave-digging the following prayer is made:

> "Earth, whose day is Thursday,
>   Receive this wine and drink,
> It is your grandchild . . . that has died,
> We have come to beg you for this spot
> So that we may dig a hole."[2]

Among the Ewe and Yoruba the earth had a powerful cult, and was associated with smallpox as its "arm" or sanction. The "smallpox juju" was prohibited in Nigeria in 1917, and the cult

[1]R. S. Rattray, *Ashanti*, p. 278.
[2]K. A. Busia, *The Position of the Chief in the Modern Political System of Ashanti*, p. 42.

has gone into retirement, only to be seen in villages or hidden under other cults. But in Dahomey earth-smallpox is still the most popular of all the ancient cults. The Yoruba have a popular farm-god, who is connected with the fertility of crops and men and comes into prominence at times of planting and harvesting.

The earth deity Ala (Ale or Ane) is the most important public and private divinity of the Ibo of Nigeria. It is more important than any of the sky gods. Ala is often seen in the wooden and clay images in which the Ibo delight; with a child on her knees and sometimes a crescent moon near her she has been compared to the Egyptian Isis with Horus, or even with some Italian madonnas. Ala is the owner of all men, quick and dead. As Queen of the Underworld she is connected with the cult of the ancestors. She is also responsible for public morality, and offences against the law are crimes against Ala who makes the law and by whom oaths are sworn. So Ala is called the unseen president of society. Every village or commune has its shrine of Ala, which is the chief of the shrines and its priest the leader of others. The shrine is usually simple, a tree with a pottery dish in which offerings are placed; sometimes stones or pieces of iron are placed there also. Public sacrifice is made to Ala before hoeing and planting the land, and at harvest. The senior priest pours out wine and addresses Ala, saying, "Your children have brought palm-wine to you. Protect them and their farms. Grant that none may meet with any untoward event, such as falling from a palm-tree."[1] At harvest all the village people attend, and the priest offers wine and yams, and makes a wave-offering of a fowl over the heads of the people.

Water Gods

Water is generally considered sacred, as in Egypt and other lands. Water is used in many rites, purification is by water and it is associated with the production of life. Christian sects make much of baptism by complete immersion, and they give water for ritual baths and medicinal drinks. They consider, as do pagans, that medicinal water must be from a spring, river or well, and not from a tap or boiled, because boiling kills the spirit in water.

[1] C. K. Meek, *Law and Authority in a Nigerian Tribe*, p. 26.

Wells, springs, rivers, lakes and the sea are believed to have spirits dwelling in them, like mermaids, and in some places great cults are made of these naiads.

The greatest nature god of the Ashanti is Tano, of the river of that name, whose fame spreads far and wide and into many places distant from rivers. Tano is the head of a pantheon and has wives, sons and brothers who are other streams and watery places. He has numerous temples and priests, some of which have been described by writers about the country.

Rattray quotes several times a piece from the traditional drum language, which shows that Tano is regarded as having had a part in creation:

"The stream crosses the path,
The path crosses the stream;
Which of them is the elder?
Did we not cut a path long ago to go and meet this stream?
The stream had its origin long, long ago.
The stream had its origin in the Creator.
He created things,
Pure pure Tano."[1]

Most tribes have cults of rivers. The Yoruba storm god has rivers for wives, one of whom is the river Niger. He is the "owner of the water of life", and in his temple are pots of sacred water. People believe in spirits in streams that have to be propitiated by those who wish to cross them or build over them. These spirits are much feared by people who go to draw water at dusk when the naiads are liable to seize the unwary.

Lakes are sacred, like Lake Bosomtwe in the Gold Coast whose decaying matter explodes sometimes, giving off gases and noises, and the lakeside dwellers believe the goddess to be active then. There is a curious legend that this lake was formerly further north, and a similar belief is held of Lake Bamblime in the Cameroons which, it is said, was previously some miles away and was transported by a powerful spirit to its present place.

The sea is the home of powerful spirits, and is often revered

[1] *Ashanti*, p. 11.

far away from the coast. The Yoruba sea god, Olokun, is represented by one of the famous Ife bronzes found many miles from the sea. People who dwell along the sea coast, and are engaged mainly in fishing, perform many rites to propitiate and bind the restless wave. Fowls, and on great occasions cattle, are thrown into the sea. In olden days human beings were sacrificed in times of crisis, some riding a bull into the sea, like Europa. Under the sea are palaces of mermen, organized into kingdoms and courts. At times they try to break their appointed limits, and memories of inundations support this. There are myths of battles between land and sea gods, in which the sea is eventually bound in chains and cast back into its abode. This is often the nearest approach to a myth of a primitive flood in West Africa.

The snake cult is frequently associated with water, rivers and sea. Snake, tree and water often figure together in cults, as in Genesis. The sacred snake is usually the python, a non-poisonous snake which crushes its prey. Because it sheds its skin it is regarded as immortal, as in the Genesis myth where it claims to know the secret of immortality. The snake is often connected with the ancestors and the underworld; sometimes it has the secret of sex.

Snake temples are found along the coastline and up the rivers. Famous temples are in Dahomey and in the Niger Delta. In the latter region the snake is often shown in carvings with a man's head, like one of the early Portuguese traders. The Dahomeans believe that the snakes are ancestors incarnate. Pythons are kept tame in temples, and if one strays into the streets people who meet it bow down, put dust on their heads, and salute it as father. It is the greatest crime ever to kill a python. If a python is found dead, it is wrapped in a white cloth and buried like a human being. Many peoples bury snakes in this way.

The snake enters into symbolism in many forms. It may be represented in rings, carved on trays, printed on cloths, or moulded on house walls. Sometimes it is depicted naturally, at other times it is symbolized by an undulating line or by one of the chain motifs common in African art. It may be painted in rainbow colours, and the rainbow itself is sometimes thought of as a snake. In some temples and palaces the snake is shown swallowing its own tail. As symbol of eternity this circular snake is found in Asian countries. On the altar in St. Patrick's chapel in Westminster Cathedral there are two snakes entwined in a circle.

Other Nature Spirits

Spirits may have their abode in any natural object, "on every high hill and under every green tree."

Hills and outstanding rocks are likely haunts of powerful spiritual forces, and many villages which nestle under these hills take the hill spirit as their principal deity. The town of Abeokuta in Nigeria is built "under the rock", as the name implies; the sacred cave of the hill spirit survives and is said to have received a human sacrifice as recently as 1941. But the cave is now surrounded by iron railings, like many a resort of tourists in Europe. At Ibadan, some fifty miles further north, the tutelary divinity of the town is a hill goddess in whose honour an annual festival is held. Trade is halted for a day in this busy modern town; fires have to be extinguished and not relit until the visit of the chief "worshipper" of the hill; there is general licence and rejoicing.

Trees may be sacred. All trees are thought to have souls of their own, and some are regarded as the dwelling-places of other powerful spirits which take up temporary abode there. Many villages have a sacred tree which enshrines the *genius loci*, and as a proverb says, "the tree may stand in the street but its roots are in the house".

The iroko tree (a sort of African oak) is sacred in most places. Sometimes it has a few pots at its foot, or it may be surrounded with a leaf fence and have a temple at its side. In any case it must be propitiated before it is cut down. Baobab trees are sacred in the interior, and are often regarded as the abode of spirits or the meeting-places of witches. Some people are associated with special trees; a man's umbilical cord may have been buried under a palm-tree which is sacred to him; he keeps this association secret lest if anyone cut down the tree his own life be endangered. Other trees may be thought of as the haunts of unborn children, and mothers pray there for offspring. Prematurely dead children may haunt groves and be a danger to passersby; children are warned not to play there. The spirits of twins are sometimes thought to turn into, or be akin to, monkeys and rites for them are performed in the forest.

In the deep bush are dangerous spirits or ghosts. These may be ancient haunts, such as Zimbabwe, uncut thickets or impenetrable bush. Here live dangerous ghosts of men who have been lost, or drowned or burnt alive and have not received proper burial. Non-human spirits are there too, grotesque dryads and demons that prey on heedless men (as in Amos Tutuola's book *My Life in the Bush of Ghosts*). Fairies may impart secret lore and medicines to hunters who have gained their favour.

The forest animals, or "people of the earth", are many of them sacred to different clans who have taboos of killing one animal or another: leopard, python, duiker, crocodile, elephant. If the animal is killed its soul must be propitiated, lest it pursue the hunter as a ghost. Some interior tribes of the Gold Coast believe that dead men rise up as certain animals. Those to whose clan the animal is sacred will say, "They are our ancestors, they would not injure us". The animals symbolize the vitality of the ancestors, and they dwell on the ancestral land. Ancestors, like animals, are restless and aggressive, and their unpredictable and dangerous character is aptly represented by the animals of the bush.

The great gods fade off into the lesser spirits, forces that are vague or of local importance only. The *lares* and *penates* of the Romans can be paralleled in Africa, and like them the African household gods may be chosen from the greater gods, or from being guardians of fields and cross-roads they may come to be watchers over households. West Africans believe in guardian demons, forces which are potent for evil but may be turned to good account, which watch over house and village, as did similar demonic and animal spirits in the ancient world.

Special societies have their own presiding spirits, crafts have their particular gods, villages have their guardians. Above these are the greater gods, who are ubiquitous, may have many temples or altars, and are not tied down to any special place. They are spiritual beings, and though anthropomorphic images may be made of some of them this does not mean that they are mere idols. The gods, small and great, are spiritual powers, which men seek to propitiate in order to avert troubles or obtain favours.

Polytheism is a stage through which many peoples of the world have passed. It is not illogical, but is the outcome of belief in the manifold spiritual powers in nature. When Rattray asked an Ashanti priest why he did not worship just one God and leave out the lesser powers, the old man replied: "We in Ashanti dare not worship the Sky God alone, or the Earth Goddess alone, or any one spirit. We have to protect ourselves against, and use when we can, the spirits of all things in the sky and upon the earth . . . If I see four or five Europeans, I do not make much of one alone, and ignore the rest, lest they too may have power to hate me."[1]

[1]*Ashanti*, p. 150.

THE SOCIAL GROUP

CHAPTER V

THE ANCESTORS

Importance of the Ancestors

"No approach to any appreciation of indigenous ideas regarding God can take any path but that through the thought-area occupied by the ancestors." So writes an authority on Nyasaland. "To us the idea of ancestral priority has just no meaning, but to these older African men and women in the backland villages, life from day to day and, we might legitimately say, from moment to moment, has no meaning at all apart from ancestral presence and ancestral power."[1]

Many others who have an intimate knowledge of African life make the same point. In South Africa, "the ancestor spirits are the most intimate gods of the Bantu: they are part of the family or tribe, and are considered and consulted on all important occasions". In Rhodesia, "the family divinities are the ghosts of one's grandfathers, grandmothers, father and mother, uncles and aunts, brothers and sisters".

So in Nigeria, "all Ibo believe that their lives are profoundly influenced by their ancestors, and this belief has far-reaching sociological consequences . . . Sacrifice has to be offered to them at regular intervals, or when a diviner indicates". In the Gold Coast, "in the everyday life of the Gã the dead are very present . . . Most people, as a regular habit, never drink, and many never eat, without throwing a small portion on the ground for their forefathers". In Sierra Leone, "prayer is normally offered through a succession of ancestors . . . Two distinct groups of ancestors are 'worshipped' . . . those ancestors whose names and feats are known . . . and those who died in the far distant past".

Thus there is no doubt that ancestral spirits play a very large part in African thought; they are so prominent in the spiritual world that they must be considered early in this book. The ancestors are part of the social group, and while no doubt

[1] T. Cullen Young in *African Ideas of God, p.* 38.

it might be more logical to lead up to them from the lower members of the living group, and then through the ranks of chiefs and kings, yet it is more convenient to reverse the process and treat of the ancestors first, and link them thus closely to the beliefs in gods and the Supreme God.

It is sometimes said that where there is a strong pantheon of gods the ancestors are less prominent, for example with the hundreds of divinities of West Africa, as if there were a kind of economy which prevented men from worshipping too many spirits at the same time. It is true that in the Ashanti wars the most popular spirits were those of dead warriors whose help was invoked, whereas the Yoruba called upon a mythical god of war. But the ancestors are important to all African peoples, though doubtless in some parts fulfilling functions elsewhere ascribed to gods, for example rain-making.

Even those peoples that believe in many gods do not distinguish them all clearly from ancestors, indeed they may have developed out of distant ancestors who have removed away from the nearer and more recently departed. The great Yoruba god of thunder is said to have been the fourth king of Oyo, and with some skill politicians seem to have imposed this ancestral-thunder worship on subject peoples as a means of binding them to the dominant royal house. A very popular oracle god is believed once to have been a wise man on earth. The other gods have myths told about them in such human wise that it is hard to know whether they are ancestors promoted to the hierarchy of gods, or divine beings who are but too human in their appetites like the Greek gods.

The Activities of the Ancestors

The ancestors are believed to have survived death and to be living in a spiritual world, but still taking a lively interest in the affairs of their families. Beliefs in a future world are varied. It may be thought of as subterranean, like Hades, or celestial, like Heaven, or in the east whence many African peoples think their ancestors originated and which is also the land of sunrise.

Yet the departed are not far away, and they are believed to be watching over their families like a "cloud of witnesses".

Everything that concerns the family, its health and fertility are of interest to the ancestors, since they are its elders and will also seek rebirth into the same family. The family land is their property, and they must be consulted when land is let out to other people.

Frazer, in *The Fear of the Dead in Primitive Religion*, says that the attitude of primitive peoples towards departed spirits is very different from that of civilized peoples. The general attitude is one of fear rather than affection. This statement needs qualification. Many civilized races fear the dead, are terrified of ghosts, and try to shut their eyes to the fact of death to such an extent that it has been said that Europeans suffer from "thanatophobia", i.e. fear of death. Africans, who have a culture of their own, not only fear their dead but also seek their help. Their attitude might best be described in the psychological term "ambivalent", as compounded of both fear and affection.

There is no doubt that Africans fear their dead in many ways. African life was not that of carefree "belles sauvages" until the white man came with his upsetting ideas and ways of life. The ancestors are ever at hand to harm or to help. The Tallensi of the Gold Coast are said to wage a never-ceasing struggle with their ancestors. "Men try to coerce and placate their ancestors by means of sacrifices. But the ancestors are unpredictable. It is their power to injure and their sudden attacks on routine well-being that make men aware of them rather than their beneficant guardianship."[1] By their attacks and interventions men come to obey the ancestors, and so the social order is maintained. The animals which represent the ancestors as totems are those that are most like them in their aggressiveness, restlessness, and ubiquity. Particularly are the "teeth-bearers", the carnivores, apt symbols of the fierceness and vitality of the ancestors.

In the southern Gold Coast we are told that no man "is half so much afraid of his gods as a man is of his ancestors . . . the ever-present watchful dead and their power to smite or bless the living".[2] And in Basutoland, "the living are actually afraid

[1] M. Fortes, *The Dynamics of Clanship among the Tallensi*, p. 145.
[2] M. Field, *Religion and Medicine of the Gã People*, p. 197.

of the dead, and if they find themselves dreaming of their kins-
men and friends or brooding over their death, they resort to
various rites to stop it".[1]

Any evils may be attributed to the ancestors. Drought and
famine are referred to them, for these affect the crops which
are their concern as growing on their land. But earthquakes, and
even thunder and lightning may be referred to the anger of the
forefathers.

More especially are sickness and death thought to be due at
times to the ancestors. They may be annoyed at the neglect of
their descendants, and special diseases such as insomnia or
epilepsy are put down to them. The ghost of some unsettled
dead person may enter a human being on earth and weaken
him. Cure would be brought about by sending the ghost away,
through a rite or medicine. Ghosts are usually thought to be
the spirits that have not received proper burial, and who are
wandering about between this world and the next.

Childlessness, one of the greatest curses to an African, may
be ascribed to the anger of an ancestor. But normally the fathers
should be interested in the growth of their own clan, not only
from a proprietary interest, but because childlessness blocks the
channel of reincarnation. So barrenness is put down rather to
the account of witches or to some inscrutable god.

Many people seem to wish to ensure that the ancestors
are kept as far away as possible. "Sleep well", one sees in many
obituary notices. But a distinction may be made between the
ordinary dead, who are buried in or near the family house,
and the troublesome ghosts who are sent away by force or fraud.
The dead of one's own family may not be so fearsome as those
of another family, who would not be bound by ties of kinship
to respect those they meet.

The ancestors are besought for benefits, albeit with fear and
trembling. They are the proprietors of the land, as elders of the
community, and alienation of the land in these days of sales
and "enclosures" are often against the ancient customary laws
which would have allowed rent but not sale. Hence trouble
arises in Kenya or in West African cocoa land disputes. The
ancestors are believed to fertilize the earth and promote the

[1]H. Ashton, *The Basuto*, p. 114.

growth of crops. They receive offerings when the land is dug, and when the crops are harvested. No man may eat of the fruits before the ancestors, as elders, have partaken of the first-fruits. Similarly in time of drought they are called upon, as having more influence with the powers that be than have lesser mortals. They may give a shower or a bumper harvest.

The ancestors are prayed to by the childless, and many a woman prays, like Rachel, "give me children or I die". This desire to multiply and replenish the earth is one of the root reasons for polygamy, and it has ensured the perpetuation of the race in times of high mortality.

The ancestors were thought to be able to help their tribe in time of war, and were invoked before battles. In particular are the ancestors believed to have acquired special knowledge in the afterworld. They are consulted as oracles, and mediums pass on their messages to those who consult them. In dreams ancestors speak to men, and the interpretation given by mediums indicates the will of the fathers. They can give new medicines and reveal new forms of treatment to doctors.

The dead may be simply glimpsed in a dream, and that merely indicates their continued interest in their sons. But if they appear angry or pleased, then action must be taken accordingly. Sacrifices of drinks, fowls or animals are made to turn away the forefather's anger, and if his grave has been neglected then the wayward son takes care to repair the damage and quiet his own guilty conscience. Pains are taken to soothe the departed spirit, by enjoining it to sleep peacefully. If this is not done, the ancestor may smite some member of the family with a sickness that proves fatal and leads that member to join him in the world beyond.

If dreams are not clear a medium is consulted. This may be done in any case, since many dreams are interpreted by opposites. To dream of death may signify joy, and a wedding-dream may be unlucky. Very often the medium has some message of his own, apart from the dream, and goes to tell a man, "Your father wants you to give him a sheep." Or the accidents and coincidences of life may be interpreted as due to neglect of the dead. Men go to a good deal of trouble to find out what the departed want.

Ancestral Rituals

Many rites, of widely varying importance, are made for the propitiation, help and repose of the departed spirits.

The so-called "human sacrifices", which shocked early travellers in East and West Africa were most often part of the ancestral rites. Often they were not properly sacrifices, since they had no gift or propitiatory purpose, but sought to provide a retinue for dead chiefs. The numbers of human victims was exaggerated. Sir Richard Burton, who witnessed such killings in the 1860's, says, "Human sacrifice in Dahome has been thoroughly misunderstood by the press and public at home . . . The king takes no pleasure in the tortures and death, or in the sight of blood—as will presently appear. The 2,000 killed in one day, the canoe paddled in a pool of gore, and other grisly nursery tales, must be derived from Whydah, where the slave-traders invented them, probably to deter Englishmen from visiting the king". He admits, however, that it would not have been pleasant to be in the capital at the time of the royal funerals, and that a foreigner would not be safe there. He estimated about eighty human victims for the Annual Customs of Dahomey.

These human victims were killed on the occasion of royal funerals and their anniversaries, and were examples of "filial piety, deplorably mistaken, but perfectly sincere". The king must not go to the underworld unaccompanied, but must have servants befitting his state. So certain pre-destined officials and slaves would be buried along with the king, as in ancient Meso-potamia. Thereafter, at the Annual Customs, another batch of victims would be sent in honour of the dead monarch, to take him messages and increase his prestige. Such customs were made on a large scale in Kumasi, Abomey and Benin, the "cities of blood", and to a lesser extent in many other towns and villages.

In Uganda human life was taken freely at different stages during the ceremonial of the accession of a new king. Some of the murders were intended to protect the king by magical benefits, and others to assert his powers of life and death. During his reign further ritual murders were made to protect him from sickness, or to cure disorders in the land. The welfare of the king was of great importance to the people, and the murders were justified as "setting the land in order". Here as elsewhere these killings were done not from lust of blood, but to gain some benefits from the flow of blood, "shedding life to enhance life".

Today, these ancient rites, where they are still performed, are done with animal substitutes. The Swazi of South Africa make an annual sacrifice of cattle at the royal graves. Selected men go to the groves, tell the ancestors all that has happened in the past year, and ask for their future blessing. Two cattle are killed and others are later sacrificed to different ancestors. The flesh of the beasts is eaten only by descendants in the kinship categories, and the feast makes a communion with the dead.

The Ashanti of the Gold Coast have ceremonies every three weeks, called "rest" or lying down, for their ancestors. Each ancestor is represented by a stool which he had in life and with which his soul is linked. Water is poured on the ground for the ancestor to "wash his hands", "soul food" of mashed yams or plantain is put in little dishes with wine before each stool. A sheep may be sacrificed and parts of the intestines smeared on and round the stools. Generally old people and officials attend these rites, and many commoners do not now go to the stool-houses except in special need.

The dead are ever-present and receive gifts on many occasions, even if there is no great annual "custom". The Kikuyu elders, like multitudes of other Africans, always put a little food on the ground for the departed spirits before eating, and at beer-drinking a little is always poured on the ground first. Women in cooking throw some porridge on the ground for the spirits.

On occasions of birth, marriage, sickness and family reunions, the ancestors are called upon. These are the family ancestors. The tribal ancestors will be invoked for rain, at seedtime, firstfruits and harvest, in fishing, hunting and war. As elders they must eat of the harvest first. As elders they give strength for the chase or the fight.

Worship or Veneration?
Many writers still speak of the ancestral cults as religious worship. "The gods of the Lovedu are their ancestors." Of the

Ba-ila, "The family divinities are the ghosts of one's grand-fathers." Of the Ashanti, "The propitiation, solicitation, or worship of ancestral spirits."

Other writers are positive that it is grossly misleading to speak of ancestor-worship. Cullen Young decries "the description of African belief (and not African alone!) as 'ancestor-worship'; a highly misleading term. Carrying, with us, a reference to existence *of a different kind* from that of man on earth, it immediately parts company with the African view." And J. H. Driberg says categorically, "No African prays to his dead grandfather any more than he 'prays' to his living father. In both cases the words employed are the same: he asks as of right, or he beseeches, or he expostulates with, or he reprimands . . . but he never uses in his context the words for 'prayer' and 'worship' which are strictly reserved for his religious dealings with the Absolute Power and the divinities. The Latin word *pietas* probably best describes the attitude of Africans to their dead ancestors, as to their living elders".[1]

The attitude of men to their ancestors may be illustrated from prayers. Dr. Kuper says of the Swazi: "Ancestral spirits are not worshipped. Swazi address them in much the same way as they speak to the living, and the word *tsetisa* (to scold) is frequently used to describe the manner of approach. Swazi rarely express gratitude when they think the ancestors are blessing them, and they are more indignant than humble when they find they are being punished . . . 'You, son of So-and-So, why do you kill us your children? Why do you turn your back on us? Here is your beast. Take it. Look after us for we are looking after you. Why did you send illness on this child? You are greedy, you are always ready to find fault'."[2]

These "scolding prayers" are often held up as examples of the familiarity of men with their ancestors. Yet they are not insults, but rather controversies that men hold with the spirits, expressing disappointment at past failures of prayers and hopes for the future. Junod gives an example of such a prayer by the Thonga of South Africa: "You are useless you gods! You only give us trouble! For although we give you offerings you do not

[1]Quoted in *African Ideas of God*, pp. 25-26.
[2]*An African Aristocracy*, pp. 192-3.

listen to us! We are deprived of everything . . . So come to the altar. Eat and distribute among yourselves our ox (it is only a hen) according to your wisdom."

Men are closer to their ancestors than to the Supreme God, and rarely do they scold the latter. But they may complain if he seems to neglect them: "As for me, Imana (God) has eaten me. As for me, he has not dealt with me as with others." Other religions have their bold laments. "Has God forgotten to be gracious?" (Psalm 77). St. Augustine pleaded with God, "Art thou mad?" Paul Verlaine repeated it, *"Etes-vous fou?"*

Whether the ancestral cult is to be regarded as religious depends on our definition of religion. If religion is defined as "a belief in spiritual beings", Tylor's minimum definition, or more fully as "faith in a power beyond man, expressed in worship and service" (Galloway), then it is hard to see how the ancestors can be excluded from that realm.

It is true, as Cullen Young insists, that "the African community is a single, continuing unit, conscious of no distinction, *in quality*, between its members still *here* on earth, and its members now *there*, wherever it may be that the ancestors are living". But he admits that "some element of enhanced power is attributed to the ancestors". Because of this enhanced power men pray to the ancestors for that which they cannot gain by their own means.

If we compare prayers made to gods and to ancestors there is often remarkably little difference between them. Rattray gave examples of both from Ashanti, and some in which ancestors and gods are called upon together in the same prayer. "Tekyia Kwame (one of the dead kings of Tekiman) . . . here is wine from the hand of Yao Kramo. He begs you for a long reign, he begs you for long-continued health, life to this town, life for the women and men . . . Ta Kora (the great god of the Ashanti) this is yours. Ta Mensa (another name for the god Ta Kese) this is yours."[1]

Perhaps the African attitude to the different classes of spiritual beings might be expressed approximately in terms used in Roman Catholic theology. *Latria* is used to denote that supreme worship which is due and accorded to God alone.

[1] *Ashanti*, p. 117.

Dulia is the reverence and homage that should be paid to saints and angels. *Hyperdulia* is used of the special homage paid to the Virgin Mary.

It might be helpful to speak of Latria for the Supreme Being alone in Africa, with Hyperdulia for the gods and Dulia for the ancestors. But many African tribes have no true worship of gods; their place is taken by the ancestors. Moreover, theologians may make their fine distinctions but the masses often do not adhere to them. Many Italian and Spanish Roman Catholics, at times, call upon their saints to help them, without any immediate reference to God. No doubt his presence is assumed always.

Do not Africans think what they are doing? Some writers have called them "pre-logical", their religion being "danced out rather than thought out". But there is always some reflection implied in the action, and there is some belief in the presence of the powers in which men trust, even when the prayers and ritual become automatic.

Perhaps Europeans are too rigid, too insistent on fitting everything into strict categories, of worship or veneration. Africans do not bother unduly about this. They are concerned with life, and how to protect and augment it. Their philosophy of forces serves as sufficient guide. They go upwards in the hierarchy of forces, from men to ancestors, to gods, to the ultimate God, convinced that if one fails another will help. They do not debate as to whether ancestors are gods, or can be prayed to or not, they know that having passed beyond the grave the ancestors have "outsoared the shadow of our night". They have acquired new powers, those powers may help men, and so men make any sort of appeal that may get succour in time of need.

CHAPTER VI

DIVINE RULERS

True Monarchies

"There's such divinity doth hedge a king." Belief in divine kingship appears in early forms of religion, and Hocart suggested that perhaps there never were any gods without divine kings. Before 3,000 B.C. the city kings of ancient Mesopotamia claimed descent from the gods, and the people looked on them as divinely-sent redeemers. In Egypt the king was the son of a god or his incarnation, and there is a theory that these "Children of the Sun" established their sway by claiming divine honours and possessing occult knowledge.

It is not surprising, therefore, to find that in many parts of Africa the king or chief is regarded with religious awe. He forms yet another link in the hierarchy of society, which passes from men to kings, to ancestors, to gods, up to the Supreme God of all. In this reverence for the king is one of the clearest links between African belief and that of the ancient world. There are enthusiasts who would trace all African religion to ancient Egypt, and some would go even further, to Arabia, Palestine or Mesopotamia. There is much exaggeration in some of these theories. But such a sober scholar as C. G. Seligman, in *Egypt and Negro Africa*, finds one of the main links between Egypt and the rest of the African continent to lie in the kingly offices and ritual, as practised not only in East Africa but as far away as the Congo and Nigeria.

Among the Bantu peoples of South Africa, the chief is not merely a head of the tribe but is the symbol of tribal unity. He is priest and magician, ruler and lawgiver, war-leader and source of wealth. The Zulu, in the time of the famous Chaka, raised the king to a godlike eminence. His person was sacred, his people prostrated themselves before him in adoration and flattered him with adulation. No better account of the life of an

African king is to be found than Thomas Mofolo's story, *Chaka*.

Of the Venda, another Bantu tribe, it was said, "not only is the Chief thus regarded as semi-divine during the greater part of his life: towards the end of it, and sometimes long before, he actually confers godhead upon himself, when after abjuring all contact with women, and putting away his wives, he performs a solemn solitary dance which makes him in very truth a god".[1]

One of the most interesting South African royal figures is the Rain-Queen of the Lovedu in Transvaal. For a century or more strange stories have circulated about this mysterious woman. She was said to be very light-coloured, and so to be of Arab or ancient Portuguese blood, or perhaps a descendant of two Boer girls who survived when the rest of their company had been massacred. Rider Haggard romanticized the queens in his book about *She-who-must-be-obeyed*. He wrongly suggested that the queen ruled in virtue of foreign blood and lived in mysterious caves that, in fact, have never been inhabited. But he correctly stressed the high status of women, pride in female ancestry, and the queen's inaccessibility. A more recent book based on rumour, *The Bush Speaks*, suggested that the queens descended from white women sold as slaves by the Arabs, ruled by their sexual attractions, and entrapped foreign chiefs with unbridled orgies, "licentious debaucheries continuously held at the rain-priestess' capital". Happily there is now a careful and scholarly study to correct these misrepresentations. E. J. and J. D. Krige are trained anthropologists, who lived among the Lovedu, and have written the definitive account of these people in *The Realm of a Rain-Queen*.

The Lovedu queens have been long-lived. There have only been three queens in the last 140 years, and Queen Mujaji III, had already lived forty-three years when the Krige's wrote in 1943. But the longevity of the queens is less important than their physical perfection. The queen should never have a day's illness, she should be immune from disease and her first sickness should be her last. When old age comes the queen performs ritual suicide; this elevates her to divinity, for she dies not

[1]G. P. Lestrade, quoted in *The Bantu-speaking Tribes of South Africa*, p. 176.

because of any mortal weakness but by her own act. The life of the country is bound up with her own. She is called "the soil". When she dies "the country dies with its owner", and many people flee the land because of the famines that are expected to follow the queen's death. The queen is primarily a rain-maker, as we shall see shortly.

Among the Swazi, the king and his mother are at the head of the hierarchy of mortals. He is called "child of the people", and she is "mother of the people of the country". When fully installed the king is called the Lion (Ingwenyama) and his mother is named the Lady Elephant (Indlovukati). The balance of power is between these two, they are both called *inkosi*, ruler. The mother is custodian of the national sacred objects, but her son must co-operate in manipulating them if they are to be effective. The king and his mother are spoken of as twins, and if there arises bad feeling between them it is believed to cause national disaster, famine or drought. The dual control of the nation by mother and son is referred back to the creation and origin of all things.

The kingship in Uganda was looked upon as so important that all the country was the king's possession, and conversely the welfare of the king was believed to be vital to the people. The king did not necessarily administer all justice, or lead in battle, or perform ritual sacrifices, but while he could delegate these powers to officials he was the final source of law and leadership. To be without a king was regarded as disastrous. For that reason, here as elsewhere, the death of a king was not announced until his successor had been appointed. Ritual human sacrifices were offered to protect the king from harm and "set the land in order".

J. H. Speke described the king of Uganda, in 1863, in his *Discovery of the Source of the Nile*. "The king, a good-looking, well-figured, tall young man of twenty-five, was sitting on a red blanket spread upon a square platform of royal grass . . . On his neck was a very neat ornament—a large ring, of beautifully-worked small beads, forming elegant patterns by their various colours. On one arm was another bead ornament, prettily devised; and on the other a wooden charm, tied by a string covered with snakeskin. On every finger and toe he had alternate brass and copper rings; and above the ankles, halfway up the calf, a stocking of very pretty beads. Everything was light, neat, and elegant."

Across in West Africa there were the well-known monarchies of Benin, Yoruba, Dahomey and Ashanti, and the emirates of the north, now much diminished in glory since the coming of colonial rule and the growth of democratic ideas of self-government. The Alafin of Oyo, recently deprived by his own people of most of his powers, was once head of all chiefs in Yoruba country, and to him homage was paid annually by representatives of many smaller kingdoms. He was held to be the direct descendant of the legendary and semi-divine Oduduwa, founder of the nation and now emblem of a national society. Another of his forbears was Oranyan whose staff turned to stone and may still be seen as one of the rare monoliths of West Africa. When the king came to power he made a ritual meal of his predecessor's heart, and to become a king was called "eating the king".

Eva Meyerowitz has recently claimed full divine honours for the king of Ashanti, the sacred ruler of the sacred state. Chosen by the queen mother and the people, the king is the terrestrial representative or son of the sun. His soul, filled with the potent energy of the sun, is the source of life and blessing to the state. As son of the sun the king is called "he who claims the beginning of time", and he still claims "I am the centre of this world round which everything revolves". The king is symbolized by the equal-limbed cross, the sign of the sun. Gold is his sacred colour, which he uses in many ornaments, and he covers his body with gold-dust during certain ceremonies.

Bowdich, the traveller who visited the court of Ashanti in 1818, described the king thus: "He wore a fillet of aggry beads round his temples, a necklace of gold cockspur shells strung by their largest ends, and over his right shoulder a red silk cord, suspending three saphies cased in gold; his bracelets were the richest mixtures of beads and gold . . . his ankle strings of gold ornaments of the most delicate workmanship . . . He was seated in a low chair richly ornamented with gold; he wore a pair of gold castanets on his finger and thumb which he clapped to enforce silence . . . The royal stool, entirely cased in gold, was displayed under a splendid umbrella."

Kingless Societies

The great monarchies, which were to be found in South, East and West Africa, were not the rule everywhere. Some societies were properly monarchical, with central authority, administration and judiciary; they were true governments. There were distinctions of status, privilege and wealth, corresponding to the distribution of authority and power. Such were the kingdoms of the Zulu, Swazi, Bamangwato, Baganda, Nupe, Fulani, Yoruba, Ashanti and many others.

There are other groups which have lacked a central authority, administrative machinery, and judicial institutions on a large scale. Here the divisions of rank, status, and wealth have been much less clearly marked. The Ibo of Nigeria and the Ewe of Togo had no widely ruling chieftaincies properly belonging to their tradition, yet no African peoples are today more nationally self-conscious or striving more eagerly towards self-government. Groups such as Tallensi in the Gold Coast, Nuer in the Sudan, Kikuyu and Masai in Kenya, are further examples of these stateless societies.

Some of these less clearly defined political groups have assimilated ideas of their neighbours. Kingship was never a feature of the Ibo of Nigeria, but it has occurred in one or two communities, for example, at the important town of Onitsha on the lower Niger. This kingship derived from the neighbouring kingdom of Benin to the west, and there are two kindreds which hold the right of succession between them and both claim origin from Benin.

Even where there was no king, or widely recognized chief, the leading person of a local group would hold the highest title obtainable, that of Eze among the Ibo. This word implied rule, and was indeed applied to God. The Eze was head of the community and exercised certain priestly functions. He was head of the judiciary and administered ordeals. Additional significance was given to this title on the coming of European colonial rule. It was a convenience for foreigners to rule through a local chief (the famous "indirect rule"), and many political disputes arose because men claimed to be chiefs, and were frequently recognized as such by the administration, when in fact they had no right to the title.

In Kenya, the Kikuyu had no chiefs in the European sense of the term. The British administration thought that throughout Africa there must be a system of chiefs and sub-chiefs, and they appointed the spokesmen of the "senior ridge councils" of the Kikuyu as their chiefs. Thus a foreign system was introduced, and it is easy to see that a government nominee might abuse his new powers and lose the respect of his fellows. The Kikuyu religious and legal leadership was exercised by the father of the extended family, and by a council of a number of extended families in a sub-clan. The head of the sub-clan officiated in large sacrifices to God and the ancestors.

Enthronement Rites

Where there are monarchies the accession of the king has been marked with ceremonies which, of course, differ considerably from country to country. Every royal Swazi babe has special rites at birth, for the heir to the throne may not be made known until the ruling king is dead. Here kingship must be in the male line. If the king dies before his successor has reached puberty then the latter has to undergo the puberty rites first, after which he is publicly installed. This done, regiments from all over the country assemble and the youth is shown to them with the words, "Here is your king". He receives royal emblems, which are few; an assegai whose blade has been washed with the gall of a black ox, a copper bracelet, and a staff that is supposed to make the holder invisible. The power of these insignia comes from their association with past monarchs.

The Swazi king is ritualized by special blood ties between himself and chosen subjects: two young men and two ritual wives. The two chief lineages each choose a youth of the same age as the king. Tiny cuts are made on the right side of the body of one and the left side of the other. Cuts are made on the king's body on corresponding sides, the blood is exchanged, and rubbed in with medicines. The medicine and the blood "are with power; they speak in the body". Similar exchanges of blood are made with the two queens chosen from special clans. The queens are called "right-hand queen", and "left-hand queen". These blood-pacts give their possessors special privileges but also special burdens. If the partner dies before the king that is regarded as an insult, and he must not be mourned until the monarch himself dies. When the king dies his blood-partners must go far away, and among some tribes in the past they were killed.

In addition to the rituals of accession there is an annual Swazi ritual, Incwala, which is the chief national ceremony. In this the king is the chief actor. This has been called a First-fruits Ceremony, but it is primarily a rite to strengthen kingship. The ritual demonstrates the dominance of the king and his followers in society. It is very complex, and for description one must refer to Dr. Kuper's book. But some of the songs then sung demonstrate the central place of the king, especially one which is regarded as a national anthem:

> "Here is the Inexplicable,
> Our Bull! Lion! Descend.
> Descend, Being of heaven,
> Unconquerable.
> Play like tides of the sea,
> You Inexplicable, Great Mountain."[1]

The Lovedu succession to queenship is not certain. After the death of a queen all fires in the country are put out and can only be relit ritually. There is an interregnum during which nobles become partisans of possible candidates to the succession. The rival claimants go to the hut where the queen has died which has two doors. They call upon the spirit of the deceased queen to decide which is to reign. The spirit opens the door to the one it chooses, and the new queen takes the axe, spear and shield of her predecessor and goes out by the other door. She may still have to flee if there is a stronger rival party, but in time she will be presented formally to the people by a councillor.

In Uganda any son of the king could succeed him, except the eldest. The late king's chief minister led the new king to the throne and said to the people, "This is your king, hear him,

[1] *An African Aristocracy*, p. 205.

honour him, obey him, fight for him". He was clothed in a new barkcloth and a calf-skin, like those worn by the original ancestor when he took possession of Buganda. He is exhorted to look kindly on the people, to deal justly and honour the chiefs. He is given spears and a shield, as a warrior, and a rod as a judge. The king was not a despot, but a constitutional monarch, whose office brought privileges but also responsibilities.

The Ashanti king is appointed by the queen mother with the high court officials, who also take care to find out the wishes of the people. Nobody can be proclaimed king unlawfully, nor without the Golden Stool which enshrines the soul of the nation. The rite of installation is private. The chief is taken to the stool-house where are the blackened stools of his ancestors. He is placed for a second upon the stool of his most renowned ancestor, and lifted up three times. Thus he rules by virtue of his relationship with his ancestors. This invests his person with special sacredness, and he is now surrounded by taboos. He may never walk barefoot, so as to come into contact with the sacred earth. On state occasions his very feet are lifted for him, one after another, lest he stumble and so bring misfortune to the state. He swears an oath of allegiance to the rules of the constitution, and performs rites for the welfare of the people as chief priest. He had administrative, executive, judiciary and military functions.

The king was not absolute and could be de-stooled. If he abused his powers then the virtue which flowed from the stool of his ancestors was broken off. This was often done by making him break one of the taboos, which violated his sanctity. The Ashanti de-stool a chief by making him sit on the ground, whipping off his sandals, or mutilating his body. The Dahomeans did the same. The Yoruba gave the chief parrot's eggs, as a sign that he must commit suicide. Even the most apparently absolute monarchies had provisions whereby the power of the king could be checked or broken.

Royal Funerals

Few things reveal the divinity of kings more than the ritual of death. This is of great variety in Africa, and we must be content with quoting a few examples only.

The Swazi, like many African peoples, believe that no one dies a natural death. Dr. Kuper writes: "In my original draft I wrote, 'Swazi believe that no king dies a natural death.' Sobhuza criticized this: 'No one, not only the king, is believed to die a natural death.' When I appeared sceptical, he called in some people from the village and put the questions: 'Do people die from sickness? Do they die without being bewitched? Do they die from old age?' One after another, the informants said that without sorcery no one died!"[1]

A Swazi king must be strong and well, and avoid all contact with death. He will never live in his predecessor's village, but builds a new one. He must not touch a corpse, approach a grave, or mourn for more than a few days. "When the king is in blackness the whole nation is without strength." When the king dies his death is kept a secret until his successor is installed; people are told "the king is busy". If the king's death were known the country would be "light", vulnerable to outside attack. Anyone saying the king was dead would be accused of "wishing to kill the country". Only the queen mother and a few intimate officials know when the king dies. The body is moved by night to the hut where the king married his first ritual queen. The corpse is kept there till the heir is announced. Meanwhile cattle are killed and roasted "to rejoice the dead". Finally on a night when there is no moon, chiefs and subjects from all over the country carry the corpse to the royal caves, and leave it there with a black goat and personal articles for the king's use. But mourning continues for three years.

The Lovedu Rain-queen is not supposed to die. She becomes divine by taking her life with her own hand. She takes poison, which contains the brain and spinal cord of a crocodile among other things. Her death is kept secret, and people still come to salute her and bring cases for arbitration. The body is rubbed to remove skin for the rain medicine. The queen is buried in a deep grave, standing upright, and facing north whence came her ancestors. The body is wrapped in cloth and an ox skin. With it are buried beads, water, a firebrand, a mat, and in olden days a male corpse. These are to help the departed monarch in the journey to the afterworld. The grave is only

[1] op. cit. p. 197 n.

gradually filled up, and the head is not covered until it has completely decomposed after six months. A year later the people are summoned, all fires are put out and ritually relit. Then the successor is chosen and installed as previously described.

An Ashanti king never dies, he goes "elsewhere". In the olden days the first intimation of his death would be the blood of victims coming from the royal bathroom. Then the queen mother would send for other predestined victims, some of whom would be strangled rather than decapitated as a privilege of rank.

It is a common custom in many parts of Africa to use circumlocutions to avoid saying that the king is dead. Phrases were used such as: "It is night", "the house is broken", "a mighty tree has been uprooted", "a mountain has fallen", "he has entered the vault of the skies".

Various types of embalming are practised, to give a semblance of immortality. Some Ashanti chiefs were laid out in state, with gold-dust filling the seven openings of the body. But later the king was put in a coffin over a pit for eighty days, so that all the flesh decomposed; then charms were fastened on to the skeleton. Some West African people remove the heads from corpses of kings (and some of commoners as well) for use in ancestral rituals. A number of Nigerian monarchs had their hearts removed to make medicines to strengthen their successors. Some northern Nigerian tribes strip the skin from dead chiefs and princes. Sometimes the intestines were removed while the body was drying, in Nigeria and Liberia. In other parts the body might be hung over a slow fire, and cuts made in the feet to drain away fluids. Swazi burial specialists squeezed the juices from the body to prevent too rapid decay. How far these attempts at embalming may owe inspiration to Egypt is a matter of debate.

The king, so often regarded as semi-divine during his life, becomes apotheosized at death, and enters the ranks of the tribal and royal ancestors. In the afterworld he is thought of as enjoying royal rank still, and hence the human sacrifices ("customs") made on annual or special occasions were to increase his retinue, send him messages about his family and tribe on earth, and ensure his continued favour to his children.

Privileges and Duties of Rulers

The position of chief is one of outstanding power and authority. He is the father of his people, and the symbol of tribal unity. He is the central figure in all national activities. His person is sacred, and many peoples bow to their chiefs still in complete submission. Even educated men may prostrate themselves to the ground before their chief. One day I was with the Oni of Ife, an enlightened ruler in Nigeria, when two young men went full length in the dust in their European clothes before him. The Oni quickly told them to get up, but the traditional prostration is continued because it is an old custom and even modern chiefs do not welcome threats to their authority. There are, however, many educated people, particularly in African towns, who do not bow or remove their shoes before the chief.

In the past it was a crime in many parts of Africa for ordinary mortals to wear clothes like a chief, build a bigger house than his, use his medicines or watch him eating. Many people still slip off their shoes in his presence. The chief's servants usually bare their shoulders and women their breasts before him. Offences against the chief were punished more severely than those against ordinary people, as readers of the life of the tyrant Chaka will know. Adultery with one of the king's large harem was punishable with torture and death.

The chief was the personification of the people and was often called by the name of the whole tribe. He had first choice of land, for cultivating or grazing. In Ashanti he was said to own the land and the gold, meaning that he was custodian of it all. He would preside over the highest courts, disburse the national wealth, control age groups, organize social gatherings, and impose the penalties of death and banishment.

In council some African kings hide their faces behind veils, speak only slowly or quietly, and have their wishes interpreted by a spokesman. In private they would eat alone, being served by favourite wives, and sometimes eating behind a curtain since the king was not supposed to need mortal sustenance.

Today many of the customs are changing. The growth of towns where traditional authority no longer runs, the coming of European imperial rule, the introduction of democratic elections, the rise of wealthy traders and capitalists, the use of European forms of justice, all have shaken the old systems. And yet some of the old ceremonial and authority remains.

Not only are there royal prerogatives, there are also royal obligations. The monarchy is no sinecure. "Uneasy lies the head that wears a crown." The chiefs were surrounded by multitudinous taboos that must have made life wearisome. As Frazer has said, in early societies the king existed for the well-being of his subjects. Does not our Queen still do so in Britain?

The duties of African rulers took up an immense amount of time, if performed conscientiously. They had to receive complaints and give ear to all subjects, whatever their rank. They had to listen to lesser chiefs, and represent the people in treaties with foreign powers. They were not absolute, and must consult their advisers. But they had to keep abreast of all affairs of importance, for nothing grave could be done without the chief.

In the past some chiefs accompanied their armies to battle and led the fight in person. Others provided the magic on which the issue of the strife depended. Afterwards they would settle the claims for disposal of the booty.

The chiefs played a great part in the religious life of the people. The chief was leader and representative of the people in the great ceremonies of the seasons, purifications, initiations and warfare. The king was to order the course of nature, and if he failed to do so could be ignominiously dismissed. His magic was of the greatest importance in tribal crises. He would usually have his own medicine-men, but they would work under his orders and supervision.

Most tribes had important councils of elders and lesser chiefs who served greatly to limit the actual exercise of the chief's power. The Bechuana say, "A chief is chief by grace of the tribe". Only by the harmonious co-operation of chief and elders would the life of the people be happy. Most chiefs, therefore, were constitutional rulers, they were subject to the law, and any attempt to act independently of it would fail. If they injured any subject they must make reparation, and could even be arraigned and punished by their own council.

There were dictators, such as Khama and Chaka, but these are the exceptions. A bad chief could be removed, and frequently was. The people could desert him, a civil war might break out, or he might be poisoned or assassinated, as was Chaka the Zulu himself eventually. However, this would only happen under great provocation. Normally the reverence given to a chief was so great that the people would put up with a great deal, on account of his noble birth and central ritual position.

CHAPTER VII

COMMUNAL RITUAL

Rain-making

To understand a religion not only its beliefs but its rites need to be studied. This has been very much emphasized in recent years, and indeed some writers go to the extreme of omitting beliefs altogether, which is absurd, for no peoples lack intellect and logic. But religion does need to be studied in action. The rites reveal the religious sentiments, as well as the doctrines of faith. The rites also help to show the relationship of religion to the structure of society.

Rain-making is one of the most important social religious activities in many parts of Africa. Rain is the focus of interest, since upon it depends the agricultural cycle. There are rain-makers in all parts of Africa, but they are particularly prominent in the drier eastern and southern regions.

The queen of the Lovedu, the mysterious "She", is called a Rain-queen in the most serious study of her realm. "The queen is primarily not a ruler, but a rain-maker, and men rely for their security, not on regimentation, armies, and organization, but on the queen's power to make rain for the tribe and to withhold rain from its enemies . . . The chief actor in the rain cult is the queen. During life, she is not merely the Transformer of the Clouds, but she is regarded as the changer of the seasons and guarantor of their cyclic regularity; when she dies, the seasons are out of joint and drought is inevitable. Her very emotions affect the rain: if she is dissatisfied, angry, or sad, she cannot work well."[1]

When rain is needed councillors tell the queen "the people are crying". Gifts are brought to her. Dances may be held, at which people neglect all their ordinary work until the rain falls. Sometimes, if the drought is prolonged, all fires are extinguished until young girls are sent to fetch water, and then fires are relit with special medicine. Or if the witches send false storms, threats are uttered against them and the queen is informed.

The queen does not work alone. She can send rain only "in agreement with her ancestors". Furthermore the queen always has a rain-maker to work with her. A renowned man is chosen who is a specialist in the art, and he receives payment for his work. Nevertheless he says that his power depends on the queen; "if the chief holds the rain from falling, the doctor cannot cause rain".

How the queen transforms the clouds is a closely guarded secret, which she passes on to her successor just before dying. Her medicines are kept in earthen pots which have varied contents; a human skull, the skins of dead chiefs and councillors, sea-water, feathers, shells, horns and roots. Rain-horns with some of the ingredients are said to cause rain when laid on the ground, or fair weather when they are hung up. The medicine may be burnt and the rising smoke is said to draw clouds to itself. Other chiefs have similar rain-pots which are kept in secret places.

The Lovedu queen is renowned as the greatest rain-maker in South Africa (though the Zulu Chaka declared that he was the greatest of all rain-makers). But there are multitudes of other rain-makers, in all parts of the continent. They are usually men, famous for their powerful medicines. Most are experts in weather lore, and they can tell when rain is a great way off, like Elijah, in the story of the storm and fire on Mount Carmel, spying a cloud as small as a man's hand. These "shepherds of heaven", as the Zulu call them, brave the storm when other men are terrified of the lightning and hail. They guard villages by their protective medicines. In drought they

[1] *The Realm of a Rain-Queen*, p. 270.

invoke the storm. They believe that there is a "bird of heaven" (perhaps a flamingo or stork), whose rare eggs form the most powerful ingredient in rain medicine.

That men seek for rain does not mean that they know nothing of the regularity of the seasons. They do not ask for rain in the middle of the dry season, but at the times when rain should fall. It is to ensure the due arrival of rain, in sufficient quantity, that rain-makers are employed. If there is drought, at an unwonted season, they are called in to stop it. Similarly, if there is too much rain and the crops are rotting, rain-makers are asked to drive the rain away.

Many methods of producing rain are tried, but most of them are based on the principle of similarity, that is to say that they perform some action like rain, in the hope that the elements will imitate it. Green branches are burnt, in order to produce great dark clouds which, it is hoped, will attract the rain clouds. Or the rain-maker crouches under a blanket over a fire, and his running sweat symbolizes the coming rain. Or the rain-maker fills his mouth with water, and squirts it into the air, with the object of inducing the rain to fall in like manner; like Elijah pouring out the water. A European writer in Togoland says that going on trek at the beginning of the rainy season, he took with him a boy who was supposed to have the virtue of stopping the rain falling. This power depended on the boy never washing. All went well and the weather was dry until the last day, when the boy got so hot and dirty that he took a bath, and immediately the rain fell. This was an application of the principle that like attracts like, water attracts rain.

Two fine descriptions of rain-making ritual deserve quotation. One is from East Africa, by J. H. Driberg: "From a new gourd-bowl was sprinkled the holy water which Alukileng (the rain-maker) had blessed and apportioned, that as its spray fell so might fall the rain also. And when all was accomplished according to the ancient ritual and the Rain song has been sung:

An arrow for the People of the Arrow.
Swift to the figs, O Pigeons of the Rain,
Hoes for the Hoers. (Gather, O Clansmen).
The flail of the thunder on the threshing-floor of God

they danced the Rain Dance till sunset with joyous solemnity, imitating with soft pattering feet the first slow thunderdrops, then, more swiftly, to the swishing of the women's skirts the rapid falling of steady rain."[1]

Then a great tribal rain-sacrifice among the Bamangwato in South Africa: "From the tribal herds choice had been made of a black bull, without blemish or trace of colour, which, after being given water to drink, was slaughtered at the grave. Many small fires were lit around the sacred spot, and the flesh of the victim was roasted. Of this sacrificial meal the chief was the first to partake, and after him, in strict order of precedence, each man, woman, and child in the throng had a morsel. It was necessary that every scrap of the sacramental food should be consumed on the spot . . . Then the people stood and worshipped, under the presidency of their chief, intoning the 'praise-songs' of their dead chiefs, and saying, 'We have come to beg rain by means of this ox, O Chief, our Father!' The rain-songs were also chanted; and the people dispersed with a great shout, 'Rain! Rain! Rain! Chief, we are dead—we who are your people! Let the rain fall!' As they wended their way homeward, they continued to make the welkin ring with their rain-songs; and . . . on the evening of that same day there was a drenching rain."[2]

The belief in rain-making and rain-stopping is so widespread that it is retained under modern conditions. A university graduate of my acquaintance employed a rain-stopper to sit in his compound during wedding festivities. It was reported that the rain fell all around, but not on the house where the marriage celebrations were going on. Modern writers justify rain-making ritual as part of Africa's ancient wisdom. This may well be true of the accumulated weather lore of the rain-maker, but not of the magical activities of the rain-stopper.

Many rain-makers discriminate in their predictions. "For long he stood silent, plucking at his beard, straining his eyes to see the furthermost hills . . . 'Here and here,' he pronounced, 'there will be an abundance of rain . . . But here' and he dipped his hand abruptly . . . 'shall no rain fall; but there will

[1] *People of the Small Arrow*, pp. 96-7.
[2] W. C. Willoughby, *The Soul of the Bantu*, pp. 208-9.

be drought and a hot, parching wind, and the earth shall crack with its heat, and the corn shall be withered in the fields'."[1]

Agricultural Rites

All African peoples have important communal ceremonies at the times of sowing and harvest. When the fields are tilled, the chief of the Venda people in South Africa calls all his friends and neighbours to till his fields first. When the hoeing is done, a pot of grain is symbolically cooked over three cooking stones on a grass fire. Some of the mixture is placed on a sacred axe and hoe, and then the chief's maternal aunt fills her mouth with water and spews it on the ground, saying, "Here is food for you, all our spirits; we give you every kind of grain, which you may eat. Bring to us also crops in plenty and prosperity in the coming season". Some of the grain is then given to the men and the rest to the women. Similar rites are performed at the field of every lineage headman, but the chief's rites are thought to benefit the tribe as a whole.[2]

An Ashanti farmer in West Africa, at the beginning of cultivation, brings offerings of a fowl and cooked yam for the spirit of the earth and his ancestors. As the blood of the fowl drips on the earth and the yam he says, "Grandfather So-and-so, you once came and hoed here and then you left it to me. You also, Earth, Ya, on whose soil I am going to hoe, the yearly cycle has come round and I am going to cultivate; when I work, let a fruitful year come upon me, do not let a knife cut me, do not let a tree break and fall upon me, do not let a snake bite me."[3]

So, all over Africa, when the land is tilled and planted, the blessing of the spirits is demanded. Then when the crop is ripe there are most important First-fruit ceremonies (not just harvests), of which the essential principle is that the spirits must eat of the fruits before men partake of them. These have been called "rites of primogeniture", since the spirits, if deprived of their priority in the hierarchy, would take revenge by threatening the harvest.

[1]*People of the Small Arrow*, p. 101.
[2]*The Bantu-speaking Tribes of South Africa*, p. 261.
[3]*Ashanti*, p. 215.

In South Africa when the first gourds become ripe it is taboo for anyone to eat of them before the chief has first ceremonially done so. A Basuto chief tastes the gourds as representative of the ancestors, and offers them a dish of new food saying, "I offer you the first grains of the new year that you may eat and be happy; eat all of you; I deprive none amongst you. What remains on the ground belongs to me and your little ones". Then the people taste the food in order of seniority, family by family and person by person.[1]

Among the Zulu and Swazi and kindred peoples there are great tribal gatherings at the time of the first fruits. The Swazi Incwala is primarily a ceremony that aims at "strengthening kingship", but in it "the sacrament of the first fruits is an essential rite in a complex series of rites". On the fourth day, the great day of the feast, is the rite of throwing the gourd. After the king or chief has been strengthened by medicines, and has proved his virility, he is now strong enough to eat of the new crops, after which the people can perform their own first fruits ceremony. After much dancing the king himself dances, and eventually tosses a green gourd at his warriors who catch it with their shield so that it does not touch the ground. This indicates that the taboo on touching the new crops has been lifted.

Among the Yoruba of Nigeria the "Yam festival" is part of the annual ritual of the ancestors, who are represented by masked and robed figures (Egungun). These masqueraders appear in the streets and dance, and visit people's houses, especially those that have been bereaved during the past years, for the masked dancers are the spirits of the dead. The new yams must be offered to the ancestral and divine spirits before men can eat of them.

To the Gã of the Gold Coast the annual feast called "hunger-hooting" is the very pivot of tribal life. All houses and stools are purified then. The entire remainder of the corn of the previous year is prepared, and sprinkled by old people and priests at the shrines of ancestors and gods respectively. The spirits are asked to come to eat and drink, and to continue their protection against disease and misfortune. After that the living

[1]*Bantu-speaking Tribes*, p. 262.

eat the rest of the food, huge masses of it if the previous year had been abundant. No food is left over. Then before the new corn is eaten some must be offered to ancestors and gods. There follows a time of rejoicing and licence. This is the agricultural new year, and people greet each other:

> "Take life, take life.
> May the year's end meet us,
> May we live to be old,
> May no black cat cross between us,
> At the end of this year may we sit again."[1]

Many similar rites can be read of in the principal source-books. Some have been followed in the new religions. But it is a pity that Christians tend to neglect the sacrament of first fruits, which has Old Testament precedent, and often follow instead the practice of celebrating harvest festivals in the autumn as in Europe.

Purification Rites

In addition to the agricultural ceremonies there are many other kinds of rite which are performed in Africa by or on behalf of the whole community. As examples we may select the purification rites which seek to cleanse the people from known and unknown evils.

The Incwala of the Swazi ends with a day of purification, when clothes and utensils from the past year are ritually burnt. The older people look on this burning as a purification and an offering to the ancestors, who are supposed to acknowledge it by sending rain. If rain does not come misfortune is feared, but if it falls during the ceremony the people continue until the ritual is ended even if they are soaked to the skin.

In some places the annual purification rites may be compared to the Roman Saturnalia, for they are accompanied with much licence.

In the Gold Coast and Togo there is an annual festival, which is a rite of-purification. One feature of this is the licence allowed on those days. Young men may say to any girl, "fire a

[1]*Religion and Medicine of the Gã People*, p. 51.

gun at me", or in olden days, "shoot an arrow at me". The girl then throws off her cloth and stands naked before him except for a belt of beads and a little cloth. The sight of near-nudity is not uncommon in this country, however, and the request is like that to unmask and kiss at a European carnival. Real immorality was punishable by law after the days of licence were ended.

There was licence of speech. Chiefs, kings and even gods might be lightly spoken of:

> "O King, you are a fool.
> We are taking the victory out of your hands.
> O King, you are impotent.
> We are taking the victory out of your hands."[1]

The reason for the licence and insults was explained to Rattray by an old high priest: "Our forbears ordained a time, once a year, when every man and woman, free man and slave, should have freedom to speak out just what was in his head, to tell their neighbours just what they thought of them, and of their actions, and not only their neighbours, but also the king or chief. When a man has spoken freely thus, he will feel his *sunsum* (soul) cool and quieted."

At the end of the ceremonies the symbols of the gods were taken to the water, scrubbed and cleaned, and returned to their shrines. Sacrifices were made and prayers offered to the gods since "the edges of the year have met".

Similar rites are found in Nigeria. In the town where I am writing the annual town festival has just been held, in honour of the goddess of the hill on which the town stands. It is a day of licence and insult; sexual phrases are shouted at visitors and passers-by. There is dancing and rejoicing, especially if the rain falls on that day. All fires must be extinguished, and only relit after the visit of the chief priest to each compound. Muslims and Christians make repeated efforts to curb the licentious words and deeds.

At Bida in Northern Nigeria the Muslim New Year is celebrated with just such ancient ritual. Boys and girls bathe in

[1] *Ashanti*, p. 156.

nakedness, and indulge in play that at other times would be strictly forbidden. There are torchlight processions and combats that frequently end in serious wounds, though these are not so serious as they were before authority stepped in to check them. The ritual acts express the death and renewal of the year. The licence comes from old fertility ritual, before Islamic days, and its aim was no doubt to encourage the fertility and propagation of the race, very necessary in view of the high mortality and adverse climate.

Communion Sacrifice

One of the great principles behind many social sacrifices is that of communion. Sacrifices may consist of libations of water, rum or beer, and small quantities of food. Or they may take the form of killing an animal, pouring out the blood on the altar or the ground, and cooking the rest for the participants. In the latter case the ceremony is a sacramental communion.

Eating together establishes a bond of unity among men. Of the Ba-ila it is said, "Eating together means union in close relationship between equals". When two Thonga brothers in Mozambique have quarrelled and wish to make reconciliation they say, "Let us eat out of the same spoon, drink out of the same cup, and be friends again". Sometimes an animal may be killed and the two men to be reconciled plunge their hands into the stomach together and eat some of the flesh.

The communion sacrifices to the family and tribal spirits grown out of human commensualism, and are a sort of replica of it. The ancestors are members of the social organization to which they belonged on earth, and even the nature gods have often links with the ancestral ranks. In many parts of Africa food and drinks are put on the ground for the ancestors before men partake of them.

Sacrifices in which food is shared with the spirits establish a covenant between men and gods. In the Bamangwato rain rite, to which we have referred, all had to partake of the flesh of the bull, in strict order of precedence. Behind the rites of first fruits is the belief that the senior spirits must have first share in the food which they have aided in producing, and which belongs to their tribe.

The portion of a flesh sacrifice that is given to the spirits is usually the blood, and sometimes also the fat and intestines. "The blood is the life." Every African understands this Levitical phrase, and Christian Africans have a greater understanding of the symbolical importance of blood than have modern Europeans. The blood contains the soul of the sacrifice, it soaks into the ground and so is absorbed by the spirits. If one presses the thinking African as to whether the god really has drunk the blood, he will say, "No, but he drinks the soul of the blood, its inner force."

There are rites which reveal little of the communion aspect. Whole burnt-offerings are made in time of distress, as propitiatory offerings to turn away the anger of the spirit, or solicit his help. Even then the officiating priest and his assistants may have some perquisites in the carcase.

In "human sacrifice" the flesh was rarely eaten. Cannibalism, in Africa, was restricted to a few tribes only. Sacrificing a human being was done to send slaves to a dead king, to avert some great evil, or prepare a most potent charm; not to establish a common meal.

When individuals make sacrifices the communion aspect is often prominent. Small gifts, like kola and other nuts, are commonly placed at shrines and graves and have a communion significance. The kola nut is a sign of friendship, if it is split in two and part handed to a friend that binds him in a union, "we have eaten kola together". So if a god is given part of a kola, the rest may be chewed by the worshipper. Or the halves may be thrown before the shrine, and the way in which they fall shows whether the offering is acceptable or not.

Temples and Altars

African religion has been despised because it possesses no mighty stone temples, witnessing to the artistic ability of past ages. There are no stone buildings at all worth mentioning, as there is little soft stone, and granite is too hard for use in a pre-mechanical age. Many mosques and churches today are built of clay. The temples, such as they are, are made of clay and are often small and crude. That is because worship goes on in the open air. Only the priests need to enter the temple.

In a hot country this is natural. After all, Solomon's temple was but a small chapel, and the worshippers prayed in the large open courts. There is little evidence of the building of temples by the ancient Aryans in India.

Some West African temples have been described and photographed by people like Rattray, Herskovits and Talbot, and reproduced in their respective works. They show small buildings, with symbolic lines in the clay and sometimes colour-wash painting. In West and Central Africa there are many carved images, brightly painted, which decorate temples. These give the impression of gross idolatry, though one often finds that the images do not represent the chief spirits but rather his assistants, or purely human figures. It is exceedingly rare to find any attempt at portraying the Supreme Being. In this respect Africans have been more reserved than Greek sculpture or the paintings of William Blake.

There are innumerable shrines or altars, from the clay mounds at which the Dogon of the western Sudan worship God, to the tripod holding a bowl at which the Ashanti pay their daily tribute to God.

Sacred trees are set aside as places of worship, such as the fig-trees where the Kikuyu worship God. Bushes and shrubs are allowed to grow around until they make a "grove". Such a "grove" or "bush" is common in many parts of Africa. Trees, mounds, and rocks are common places for sacrifices. Where the spirits have no temple, but are vaguely thought to live in a forest or on a hill, stones of the place may serve as altars, as for Jacob at Bethel.

The ancestors, of course, are "worshipped" at their graves. Here gifts may be made, ranging from the milk which the Cow Fulani pour out at the new moon, to the great bull which the Zulu offer in a drought. The ancestor may be thought to live in the spirit-world, but his spirit can still be invoked at his burying-place. Hence the tribal cemetery is a dreadful place.

Where there are priests they are guardians of the temples, and intermediaries for those who bring gifts. They may have several assistants to help them. Or a temple may be a private shrine for a chief. Small shrines abound in West Africa; little clay huts, often no more than three or four feet high, covered with broken thatch, under which the priest has to crouch to place his offering on the altar. Many of these shrines have an air of neglect, but they are furbished up and their images given a new coat of paint at annual ceremonies or when a generous donor makes a contribution. It is only the romantic museum collector who imagines that by keeping the image in the dusty state in which he found it he is retaining the original atmosphere. The believer paints his images when he gets money to do so.

Families often have little shrines, sacred trees, or piles of stones in their compound. Here the father of the family stands at dawn and mutters a prayer. Or he may turn to the rising sun and salute the God of heaven without any sacrifice, temple or priest; a worship "in spirit".

CHAPTER VIII

PERSONAL RITUAL

WHEN one comes to consider the rites that surround the principal events in the lives of individuals, one is almost over-whelmed by the mass of evidence. Most writers on the different African peoples have given considerable time and space to description of the stages of individual development. One cannot hope to give here even an approximately adequate picture; one can only underline some of the general features, and refer those interested in particular tribes or customs to the biblio-graphy.

Since Arnold Van Gennep, in 1909, published his study of *Les Rites de Passage*, it has been realized how important are these "traditional rites" which mark stages in the life of the common people. The transitional rites indicate the passage from one place or stage in life to another. Like some of the seven sacraments, these mark the turning-points in life: birth, puberty, marriage and death. They are accompanied with various religious or magical acts.

Birth

The ritual of birth begins with the pregnancy of the mother. African peoples recognize the act of sexual intercourse as necessary for conception, though its working may be misunderstood. The semen is sometimes thought to provide the spiritual part or vital essence of the child, and the mother's blood to give the body. Some people think that mother and father each pass on a clan soul, and the child's resemblance to a grandparent on either side may be taken to show that he is the reincarnate ancestor.

Children are greeted with joy throughout Africa. Desire for children is a main cause of polygamy and of changing one's married partner after trial has proved sterility. Any religion or medicine that promises offspring is sure of popularity. To have many children, especially sons, is a sign of wealth and prestige. Africans cannot understand why so many European couples seem to prefer to remain childless, and they regard this as unnatural, as indeed it is. The African attitude to life is world-affirming, not celibate; they share this attitude with the Hebrews between whom and Africans there is considerable affinity, as witness the way in which many Africans have adopted the Bible as their guide.

So when a woman announces to her husband or mother that she is pregnant there is rejoicing, and precautions are taken to ensure normal gestation and delivery. These precautions include both medical and spiritual attention. A sacrifice of thanks is made to the Supreme God, or the family gods or ancestors who are naturally interested in the reproduction of their family and the provision of a channel of rebirth. Prayers are offered for the health of the mother and her baby.

At the same time taboos are placed upon the expectant mother, so as to protect her from harmful influences. She may be smeared all over with white or other powder. She wears protective amulets which have the virtue of helping delivery. She avoids doubtful foods. In many places it is forbidden for her to have any knots in her clothing, since they would "tie" the birth. The husband also has some taboos, and even in towns an educated man may leave off ties and shoe-laces during his wife's confinement.

There is a general taboo of intercourse between wife and

husband for some considerable period, if not during the whole of pregnancy, at least towards the end and lasting on for two years or more after the birth of the child. The usual idea is that intercourse will harm the child, and cause the mother's milk to dry up. The weaning period is late, for few can obtain or afford cow's milk and infant foods. This long period of abstinence is a great strain on the husband, and he often takes another wife at this time. Often he only has the two wives, and births of children are spaced out conveniently. At least this bigamy is better than resort to prostitution, and the latter phenomenon is mainly found in modern towns.

When the time of confinement comes the woman frequently goes to her mother's home, perhaps for several months. The birth may take place, in South Africa, on the grinding-stone, the symbol of women's work. Prayers and medicinal leaves are used to help delivery. Doctors are rarely called in, the women of the family assisting as midwives. Men and people in a state of impurity, such as menstruation, are excluded from the hut. "The child would be ashamed to be born before a man." If the birth is difficult, as it frequently is (contrary to the European superstition that Africans have few physical and mental troubles), then it may be ascribed to various causes. Sin on the part of the woman, adultery or theft, is a common accusation for a delayed birth. If the mother confesses the name of a lover then the child may now "consent to be born". Witchcraft or sorcery may be looked upon as the cause of prolonged labour, and especially of a still birth.

When the child is born it is hailed with great joy throughout the village. The placenta and umbilical cord may be buried in the bathroom, to keep them cool, or near a tree which becomes sacred to the child. The child is washed with unboiled water, since boiling kills the power in water, and its hair ("ghost hair") is shaved off.

The child often receives a name at once. Those peoples that have a seven-day week call the child first by the day of its birth. Others give it a name according to some special circumstance of birth or place in the family: one of a twin, one born after twins, born with a caul, with the cord round its neck, feet first, with extra fingers, with face downwards, at the new year, on a holy day, with the mother dying at birth, when the father is away hunting, and a number of other occasions.

Some children are lucky, often the third, sixth and ninth. Others presage disaster or strangeness, especially twins. Twins were killed, in some parts, probably because their similarity to an animal's litter suggested that they were not human. Even people who did not kill twins, such as the Yoruba, regarded them as akin to monkeys. Some tribes have a cult of twins, by a reversal of the taboo against them. Sacrifices may be made constantly to the spirits of still living twins, and if one dies his twin will continue the cult. The curious belief is widespread that the second twin is the elder, because he sends the first before him as a servant: as in the story of Jacob and Esau and Tamar's children.

In some places, notably Ashanti, a child is neglected for the first few days of its life, for fear that it is a ghost child come to deceive the parents. If it survives this hard treatment then it is clearly a human child. There is great fear of evil spirits which harm new-born babies, and for this reason some peoples give the child a scornful or disguised name, so that it may not appear of importance to the enemy power. There is high child mortality in many parts of Africa. If a mother has a succession of children which die she may think that the same child is being born again and again, perhaps an evil ghost come to harm her. So a dying child has a mark made on its body in order to be recognizable if it is born again. Babies of such a mother are loaded with protective charms, bracelets, necklets, girdles and anklets, which make a noise or exercise power to drive away evil. All children have some protective amulet to help through sickness and teething troubles. The Thonga of Mozambique say, "the child grows through medicine".

A few days after birth, often the seventh or eighth day, the child has a naming ceremony. The relatives gather round and the child may now leave the room of birth for the first time. It receives a personal name, which marks its ritual entry into the family. Prayers are offered and libations poured on the ground for the ancestors or Mother Earth. The child may be taken to the grave of a dead grandfather and shown to him, especially if he bears the ancestor's name.

The custom of showing a child to the moon is widespread. The Gu women of Dahomey throw the child gently up in the air at the new moon, nine times for a boy, seven times for girls: "look at the moon little one". And far away in South Africa, the Basuto and Thonga show the child the moon and say, "there is your father's sister".

Should an infant die it is buried with little ceremony, especially if it dies before the naming ceremony. It is regarded as not a real person, and the mother makes a pretence, at least, of not caring for it. This is done to deceive the witch that has killed the child. The older the child the more it is mourned.

As the child grows it is educated by its mother in the early years, but it may soon learn to eat with children of the same age, and enter into their age-set. But there are few special rites until this period is left behind.

Circumcision is practised widely over Africa, but the areas of its distribution are uneven, as are the times of its infliction. Some tribes do not circumcise at all. Others practise it "on the eighth day". Many others leave it till manhood is approached, and regard the uncircumcised as still boys. Discussion of circumcision comes under puberty rites.

Puberty

Puberty is the great transition between childhood and physical maturity, and is therefore an occasion for considerable ritual. The essential principle throughout is to make the child into an adult, a full person, and to introduce him or her to sex life.

Instruction in behaviour, tribal custom and religion may go on for years before the arrival of puberty. This instruction was increased and made more explicit in the initiation ceremonies, and without passing through such rites young people could not take part in the adult life of the tribe. In our day many of these customs are on the decline. Missions have opposed pagan or immoral customs, though sometimes substituting christianized initiation rites of their own. Modern life and ways have thinned down other customs to a minimum; often the performance of circumcision is the sole remaining rite. Dr. Leakey says that "education and many other factors have reduced the initiation

rites of the Kikuyu to nothing more than the hurried performance" of circumcision. In this abandonment of character and
tribal training he finds "just one more underlying cause of the
present sad state of affairs in the Kikuyu tribe."[1]

Circumcision is often the first rite in the process of initiation.
The boy is stripped and must not show fear, else he is gagged.
The operation is crude and unhygienic, but may be performed
during a cold period of the year when wounds heal quickly.
The operation may be done by a masked figure, or in his
presence, as representative of the ancestral spirits.

Female circumcision frequently accompanies that of boys.
Clitoridectomy, or even mutilation of the labia, is found from
South to West Africa. It is difficult to find any reason for continuing this harsh custom, and missions have opposed it. In
Kenya African Christian sects have sprung up which still allow
the practice. Anthropologists, too, have opposed clitoridectomy,
and Rattray in the northern Gold Coast said that this was one of
the few instances where government should interfere with
traditional practice and prohibit it, because of the needless
suffering and danger to life caused to young women.

Many African peoples have "societies" or "schools" for
training adolescents, from the Poro and Sande societies of
Sierra Leone, to the circumcision schools of Basutoland and
Bechuanaland. In these schools young men and women,
separately, live in community and undergo hardships which aim
at introducing them to and fitting them for life as adults. There
are hard tasks to be done, exercises, severe beatings with sticks,
eating of dry or even disgusting foods, in order to teach obedience
to the elders in charge.

Training in the puberty schools involved instruction in the
mysteries of sex. Songs and dances are learnt which refer to the
sexual functions. The organs may be enlarged, but intercourse
is prohibited. In the past, chastity at marriage was highly prized,
and its lack in a bride brought shame to her family.

In some places, such as among the Ibo of Nigeria, there
are "fatting-houses" for girls. Here maidens are secluded for
months, fed on fatty foods, and their bodies anointed with oil,
so that they become as buxom as possible. Plump married

[1]*Mau Mau and the Kikuyu*, pp. 23-4.

women are considered the most beautiful, contrary to modern European views.

The "secret societies", renowned in Africa, are frequently connected with the initiation schools. Sometimes they are mummers, men or women disguised in robes of grass or reeds, with headpieces carved in wood or bearing horns. These chase the initiates, and perhaps simulate intercourse with them. They represent the power and authority of the elders, living and dead.

The noted Poro society of Sierra Leone is a male organization, with a corresponding Sande society for girls. The Poro is highly developed, ostensibly under the control of spirits who are represented by masked figures, behind whom is a staff of hereditary officials. Every male must belong to the Poro, and in his initiation he is equipped for his part in community life. Initiates are said to be swallowed by the Poro spirit when they enter, being separated from their families as by death, and at the end of the training they are "delivered" by the spirit and "born again".

This idea of rebirth is characteristic of many of these initiation rites, and is seen also in the training of some priests. The youths withdraw from the world, live a communal life, endure hardships, undergo rites which initiate them to adult mysteries, are directed by masked spirits, are given new names, sometimes even learn ritual dialects, and eventually emerge in new clothing and are restored to their families as born again to adult life.

The new names and new personalities may be paralleled by the rites of other religions. In some places, particularly East Africa, Christians have experimented with purified forms of initiation ceremonies for their converts. The analogy to baptism and confirmation is too clear to be missed.

Marriage

Those who approach the study of African marriage customs for the first time, may be surprised to find that there is not the ceremony surrounding it that one might expect. The religious element, at least, appears small and the wedding itself but a detail in a process of social arrangements.

There are two main reasons for this. Firstly, marriage is the sequel to puberty rites. The aim of initiation being to prepare for sex life, marriage is its logical outcome. Girls, in particular, may marry any time after the completion of the puberty rites, the sooner the better. The girl may have been bethrothed since childhood, and only a few token gifts remain, with wine to be offered to the ancestral spirits.

Secondly, marriage in Africa is a social affair, concerned as much with the contracting families as with the man and wife. The highly individualistic, and often irreligious, form of many modern European marriages, with two people uniting without the appearance of the families, and strangers as witnesses, would be incomprehensible to most Africans. The instability of such marriages, and the high divorce rate, would be taken by them as inevitable.

It has often been said that African husbands and wives have no choice in their marriage. Customs vary from place to place. A Basuto will know from childhood that he is expected to marry his mother's brother's daughter. An Ashanti also will be blessed if the closest type of cross-cousin marriage can be effected. But a Kikuyu chooses among his dancing partners the one who he thinks would make him the best wife. And many other tribes practise exogamy, namely marriage outside the family and even away from the village.

Whatever the amount of choice, the marriage arrangements are made by the families concerned. They may have contracted these since the childhood of the partners. But if the proposed partners have a violent objection to the union, it may still be possible to break off the agreement, if past gifts are returned. The idea of romantic love, so often exaggerated in Europe, is secondary in Africa, and one Nigerian writer declares that "love as understood by the European does not exist in Africa". Kissing was not known, though it is spreading from the gross examples seen on the films. But this does not mean that husband and wife may not grow to have a very real affection for one another, perhaps as durable as a European marriage when the gilt of romance has worn thin.

The payments made in African forms of marriage have frequently been misunderstood by Europeans, and have been regarded as selling the wife. The husband and his family transfer goods or money to the wife's family, but the words used are quite distinct from buying and selling. The transaction does not give the husband unlimited rights over his wife, she may claim divorce for ill-treatment. Many African women are very independent people.

The words used are difficult to translate accurately into English. The South African *lobola* is not quite the same as "dowry", for the woman does not dispose of the cattle given for her; but the word dowry is preferable to others. "Bride-price", "bride-wealth", "marriage insurance", have been suggested. The last expresses the idea that the purpose of the transaction is to regularize and stabilize marriage, but this word is not a literal translation. If the full dowry is paid it usually ensures that the children of the marriage belong to the husband, whereas if it is not paid they are not his even if he is their father. In these days high money payments are often demanded as dowry, and many other gifts to the bride's family as well, at ruinous cost to the bridegroom. These excesses are reprobated by the older men, who see them as distortions of the original gifts.

The basic payment in marriage used often originally to be quite small, consisting of gifts in kind, together with libations to the ancestors. This small religious action was essential to ensure the approval of the dead elders of the family to the marriage.

The final wedding rites vary. The bride is dressed in her best, goes to her husband's house in procession, is often lifted over the threshold and given a ritual bath as sign of entry to a new life. There are usually no temple ceremonies, though she may visit the graves of her husband's ancestors with him.

Death

The ritual surrounding death is long and complex in most places. The great aim of much time and expense is to ensure a proper funeral for the departed, so that his spirit may be contented in the world beyond, and will not return as a dissatisfied ghost to plague his family. Funerals are the last transitional rites, introducing a man into the world of spirits.

Bodies are usually buried as soon as possible after death, because of the putrefaction of corpses in hot countries. Photographs are often taken today of the dead man surrounded by his family, the corpse is propped up and dressed in its best. The burial of chiefs, which have already been mentioned, are more elaborate than those of commoners. At chiefs' funerals human beings might be killed, but more rarely with ordinary men. Chiefs are buried in royal graves or sacred groves. Commoners are often interred in their own houses, under the floor of some room; a practice found also in ancient Mesopotamia and other parts of the world. In South Africa the hut may be destroyed after the funeral, or the kraal wall pulled down.

After death the corpse is washed, shaved of all hair, and then dressed in the best robes and trinkets and visited by relatives. At the interment various objects are put in the grave; weapons, tools, utensils, tobacco, food, drink, beads, or money. These are meant for the use of the deceased on his journey to the world beyond, and so that he should not appear before the ancestors empty-handed. It is widely believed that the dead have to cross a river, like the Styx, before arriving in the underworld.

When the body is placed in the grave prayers may be made asking the deceased's spirit to give blessing and not harm. His soul is thought to leave the body as the earth is put in. Great attention is given to prevent the earth from falling directly on to the body. In some places a shelf is dug in the grave at the side, on which the body is placed. Others place branches or grass over the body to protect it. Formerly winding-sheets and mats were used. Nowadays coffins are increasingly popular.

In addition to the interment there is usually a later ceremony sometimes called the "second burial", or a purification rite "to make the grave firm". The time at which this is held varies very much. It may be anything from a few weeks to a year or more. As there is much expense involved the rite may be delayed, but if the ghost of the dead man is believed to become troublesome, and to appear in dreams, then the complete rites are hastened.

It is at these funeral ceremonies that some of the "secret societies" again appear. The Egungun society of the Yoruba of Nigeria consists of masked figures who represent the dead. They enter the house of the deceased, imitate his voice, receive gifts, and bless his widow and orphans.

The varied rites of funerals aim at separating the dead person from his earthly family, although he will now be invoked as an ancestor. His widows and personal property are similarly separated. His personal belongings and images may be destroyed or purified. His widow is in mourning for some months. She may remain unwashed, dressed in old clothes, and sleeping in a different place each night. This is to deceive her husband's ghost lest it return to have relations with her, which would be dangerous. During this mourning period she must remain chaste. Eventually she will bathe, dress in her best, and remarry, often being inherited by one of her husband's family.

CHAPTER IX

SACRED SPECIALISTS

In all religions one finds experts in religious matters, whether full-time or not. The sacred is dangerous to ordinary mortals, its demands are mysterious and perhaps its character capricious, so that intermediaries are needed who themselves partake of the divine nature.

There is a great deal of confusion over the names to be given to the religious specialists in various parts of Africa. Just as the words "juju" and "fetish" have been applied to a great variety of spiritual entities, so have titles such as "witch-doctor", "sorcerer" and "juju-man" been wrongly used of religious officials.

Priests

The word priest is properly used of an official servant of a god, and he normally ministers at a temple. It follows that such priests are to be found in those places where there are gods worshipped, with temples to which offerings are brought. This is mainly in West Africa.

In the cults of the West African gods there are priests who are highly trained to do their work. These priests are often set aside from birth, or they may be called to the service of the god by being possessed by his spirit. They will then retire from their families and public life, and submit to the training of an older priest. The training normally lasts several years, during which time the novice has to apply himself to learn all the secrets of consulting and serving the god.

The training of a priest is an arduous matter. Contrary to the rumours of immorality spread by some globe-trotters, the priest in training has to observe chastity and strict taboos of food and actions. He frequently has to sleep on a hard floor, have insufficient food, and learn to bear hardship. He is regarded as married to the god, though later he may take a wife. Like an Indian devotee, he seeks by self-discipline to train himself to hear the voice of his god. He learns the ritual and dances appropriate to the cult, receives instruction in the laws and taboos of the god, and gains some knowledge of magical medicines.

Women may be priestesses, and frequently they are as prominent as men in the conduct of religious affairs. The psychic abilities of women have received recognition and scope to a mu greater degree in African religion than they have in Islam or Christianity where women are still barred from the priesthood.

African priestesses may work in conjunction with men, like the Hebrew prophetesses Huldah and Anna; or they may have complete charge of a sanctuary, like Deborah, to which men as well as women may come. The training will be under the charge of an older expert, who may train several priestesses at the same time.

Priests are often recognizable by their dress. White is a favourite colour, and is sacred. Blue is also seen, and other colours. Some priests have their bodies smeared with lines in white or red chalk. Their hair is shaved in various patterns. They may wear symbolical ornaments, or a great variety of charms and amulets. Some priests dress very simply and say that charms "spoil the gods".

In the ancestral cults the chief person to offer sacrifice is normally the oldest of the village, or the chief, as the senior living representative of the ancestors. These elders are called priests in some places, and the succession of priesthood then passes down in the same family group. But such elders are not full-time or highly trained in the way in which priests of gods are trained.

The chief is a priest of his people, for he is a sacred person, and is the one charged with approaching the ancestors on behalf of the tribe. As next to them in the hierarchy of powers he is the natural link between the living and the powerful spirits of dead chiefs and elders. But the chief may have some specialist to help him in his work or propitiation, who will instruct him in the ritual and medicines to be used.

Mediums

Connected closely with the priests are the mediums or devotees, who are "possessed" with the spirit of a god or ancestor. Such people, of whom probably the majority are women, may be attached to any temple or place where men come to consult an oracle. Like the ill-named "witch" of Endor the medium proceeds, as in a spiritualistic seance, to get under the control of a spirit and give messages from the spirit world.

Priests themselves may be possessed, in some parts of Africa but not in others. Sometimes they prefer to have a number of mediums under their control, who are consulted by order and whose possession is carefully regulated. The mediums may thus be dependent on a priest. Very frequently they set up as free-lances, and go into trances when being consulted by those in need of guidance.

The mediums often have a hard training to undergo. After the initial possession, which may come upon them spontaneously at a dance, they exert great efforts, and endure privations, in the attempt to induce the return of spirit possession. For times of varying length the medium tries to produce coherent messages in a state of trance. These will often be almost unintelligible at first, but gradually they become clearer till they can be produced at will while the medium is in a genuine trance.

In parts of West Africa, especially Dahomey, there are communal training centres for mediums and assistants to priests, called cult-houses or "convents". Here the novices are secluded for months or years. The entry to the cult-house is generally preceded by an acted ritual of death, to symbolize the death of the neophyte to the world. Finally there is a resurrection to a new life. When the mediums emerge at the end of their training they come out into the world as new personalities, they speak a new ritual language, bear new names, and profess to be returning home from a distant country.

The spirits believed to possess the mediums are very varied. Mediums may impersonate the type of god they represent, strutting like a warrior, waddling like a pregnant woman, or barking like a dog. The mediums dress up to fit the part, and have their special regalia, with bracelets and other ornaments which are put on when the beating of drums has induced the ecstatic state. In their heavy necklaces and adornments of cowrie shells and seeds, and many other accoutrements, they are impressive to look at.

There is a clear difference between mediumistic possession and that of seizure by evil spirits who come to trouble man and make them ill. Many tribes do not think that ancestral spirits possess men, but rather accompany and control them, giving messages through them. The spirit is not an alien invading force living permanently with the medium, but it only comes occasionally. On the other hand people are believed to become sick when some troublesome demon comes to take up its abode in them, and the assistance of a doctor is sought to cast out the evil.

Diviners

A diviner or soothsayer is a specialist who seeks to diagnose disease, or discover the solution to problems, by means of inspiration or manipulation of objects through various techniques. Such men are very numerous throughout Africa.

Diviners are closely akin to mediums and certain priests, because they may be subject to possession and give their answers by recourse to an oracle. A man may suffer from fits or sickness, and deduce from this that a spirit is seeking to speak through him. Normally he will have dreams and visions so that, as the Zulu say, he becomes "a house of dreams". Then he wanders about and lives by himself. He hears voices calling him, or sees blurred faces of dead relatives. He then apprentices himself to an older diviner to learn his technique and get some of his worst symptoms cured. Thereafter he has to observe taboos of many foods and scrupulously avoids any defilement. He uses medicines to cleanse his body, and strengthen his inward vision. He makes great efforts at concentration, so that he becomes abstracted and sees things far away, and he comes to interpret the visions that cloud his eyes. He learns the special rhythmical dances of the possessed, and sings songs which are taught him, and others that he invents and uses as his own peculiarity. Assistants must drum and beat time for him, so that the inspiration is maintained once it begins to appear.

Diviners learn how to use drugs and treat disease. Where there is a system of divination, by manipulation of nuts or stones, they spend much time mastering the details and their interpretation. Mention of these techniques will be made in the next chapter. Frequently tests are made of the novice's powers of perception by the master hiding some object and making the pupil find it. Whether the spying-out is done by subterfuge, or under the pressure of some sub-conscious urge, may be debated. Many diviners are shrewd people, with a great store of common sense and ability to judge people and situations.

The final rite in the initiation of a diviner is generally one of purification and admission into a select company. It is a true transitional rite, an ordination sacrament, in which the novice passes from the preparatory stage to that of fully-fledged expert. The body is cleansed with medicines, the new diviner is furnished with amulets, endowed with drugs and their secrets, and recognized by his fellow-diviners.

In village life the diviner is an important figure, consulted on many occasions in life. He is a "medicine-man", and often also a "witch-doctor". He deals in drugs, most of which however have a magical rather than pharmaceutical value. He diagnoses the spiritual cause of the disease, and does not consider it as purely physical. By means of his bones or nuts he may tell fortunes, reveal the past, predict the future, find lost articles, or discover thieves. He is the wise man of the village, and beyond the superstitious there is a fund of knowledge of character and of gossip that enables him to draw correct conclusions.

Herbalists

There is overlapping between herbalists and diviners, who may both be "medicine-men". But the "men of the trees" often have the widest knowledge of the curative properties of herbs, plants, bark and roots. Many of them are hunters, whose long experience of forest life has introduced them to little-known plants. Their secrets may be handed down from other hunters and experts. But the mystical elements can never be completely excluded, for many of them claim to have received their secrets from fairies and forest spirits who have befriended them, and these may even have made a pact of exchange of blood with the hunter.

The medicines in which herbalists deal are very varied, and if one examines their bags one finds many different types of medicine. One writer on the Zulu says, "there are baked insects and dried reptiles; the dung of lions in powders and the fat of the water-sprite in bottles . . . skins and bones of every conceivable animal, and hundreds of barks, roots, berries, leaves —in a word, choice selections innumerable and wonderful, medicinal and magical, useful, harmful, and inert, from the whole range of mineral, vegetable, and animal kingdoms, terrestrial and marine."[1]

It is not easy to find out why certain remedies are used. They may have been prescribed by the herbalist's own master. Or they may have some fancied resemblance to the symptoms of the disease; like the American negro Voodoo priest who uses "red clover for cancer, dock for liver trouble, boneset for fever".

It has been the custom for Europeans to dismiss these remedies as purely superstitious. In our day, Africans are claiming that their medicine-men know many ancient remedies of which European medical science is ignorant. There is no reason to doubt that there is some truth in this. It is certain that scarcely any serious attempts have been made so far to analyse the medicines used, and many herbalists would not be willing to submit their collections for analysis. But one should not therefore assume that all herbalist's medicine is necessarily good. There is undoubtedly a good part of superstition, mingled with the remedies that are chemically valuable.

[1] A. T. Bryant, *Zulu medicines and medicine men*, p. 11.

Many of the most popular medicines are purgatives, and emetics are also common. Other methods of treatment include poultices, ointments, rubbing powders, sweating baths, and blood-letting. There are specialists who have their own technique for particular types of sickness: men who doctor sores, treat abscesses, or heal fevers. Some of the religious cults had the aim of curing specific diseases. There are smallpox gods in West Africa whose priests isolated the sufferers and treated them for the disease. If death ensued then all the belongings of the deceased would be destroyed by the priests. Forms of inoculation against smallpox are still practised by diviners in the Sudanese areas.

We have already referred to rain-makers, the "shepherds of heaven". The solitary training of one such may be quoted: "He grew thin and gaunt during those three years, and his eyes glowed like stars from their sunken sockets. But he learned the ways of all the winds and became familiar with strange birds and animals. The rare heron which flew from the far eastern lakes, its white wings fringed with purple, told him of coming storms: the different cries of the peewit carried their peculiar warning . . . He could read the stars and every night the moon shared its secrets."[1]

Witch-doctors

The term "witch-doctor" is one of the most abused in European writing about African beliefs. Frequently regarded even by legislators as a witch, an evil man seeking to poison his neighbours, or a perverted priest, the witch-doctor is really none of these things. He is a fully recognized and highly respected member of society. His function is not to harm but to heal, and to release from their pains those who believe themselves to have been bewitched. It is against the evil activities of nocturnal witches that the doctor operates in the public interest.

Disease in Africa is normally regarded as having some spiritual cause. Because they neglect this side of life European hospitals are suspected, and regarded as cold and inhuman. Not only disease but death itself is thought to be due to an evil

[1] *People of the Small Arrow*, p. 94.

spiritual force. The idea of natural death is foreign to many peoples. "An enemy hath done this thing."

Among the most powerful evil influences that are supposed to cause disease and death are the witches. The nature and extent of the belief in witchcraft will be considered later. Here it is sufficient to say that witch-doctors are what the name literally says, namely, doctors of those who have been bewitched. They seek the healing of those people whose souls are believed to have been injured or removed by witches. Hence witch-doctors are the chief agents in a curative campaign, and are benefactors of society, in intention at least. As one writer says, the witch-doctor "is no more a witch than an Inspector of the C.I.D. is a burglar".

Yet it is true that the witch-doctor has certain affinities with witches, for he has something of the same spirit, by which he can perceive the evil activities of others. As another authority says, "Only by Beelzebub can one cast out Beelzebub". The power of witchcraft may be controlled, and only if it is perverted is its owner ruined. If he gets a taste for blood then the power will turn against him. Hence the witch-doctor must be an upright man, else he would destroy himself.

The witch-doctor may be a specialist in bewitching alone. Very often he is also a diviner and a dealer in good magic and herbs. He may manipulate stones to predict the future or to detect witches. He may go into a trance and with an aroused second-sight be able to point out those who are harming their neighbours. That perhaps they are not doing so does not detract from his conviction that they are engaged in evil ways. Some witch-doctors claim to be able to recognize witches by special signs: they have hairy faces, bleared eyes, or red smoke coming out of their heads. But to see these marks one must have "the right sort of eyes".

The training of witch-doctors is long and complex. The best description has been given by Professor Evans-Pritchard in his book on the Azande people of the Nile-Congo divide. Azande witch-doctors are usually men, and they are united by bonds of mutual assistance but not into a close corporation. The pupil apprentices himself to an older man for varying periods, paying him fees, and later going round to other experts to learn their peculiar secrets. The novice learns the use of magical potions and ointments. He attends seances of witch-finding, and watches the methods used. So he slowly finds out how to discover witches, and how to protect himself against their attacks.

The chief rite in the Azande initiation of a witch-doctor is a ceremony of public burial and resurrection, a transitional rite The neophyte is prepared for this by observing chastity and certain taboos on food. He is loaded with medicines and placed in a shallow grave, out of which however both his head and feet protude. The performing doctors dance around the grave and divine the candidate's success. Eventually the novice is raised up and rests while more medicines are applied to him. At the end he is fully dressed in official costume and dances with the others. He takes a new name and sets up now as a new person, with a professional name appropriate to the custom he hopes to attract.

Seances of witch-doctors are held whenever people feel troubled by witchcraft, or when a rich man wants to call the doctors together for a public display at his house. The witch-doctors come dressed in their regalia; somewhat skimpy dress but multitudes of packets containing magical medicines and ornaments to help them in the dance: whistles, rattling gourds with seeds, bells, anklets, bracelets, armlets, girdles. A circle may be drawn on the ground into which the doctors alone may enter, horns containing medicines are stuck in the line of the circle, and there may be a pot of water in which the doctors "scry" the witches.

Dancing takes place to the accompaniment of drums, and in many parts this is the means by which excitement and ecstasy are produced. A doctor will dance alone for a time and consider a question that has been put to him by a man in the audience. When he stops he speaks in a far-away voice, as if the reply came from somewhere else. If the answer is not explicit he dances again more furiously, perhaps cutting himself with a knife, like the priests of Baal. This is the type of sensational dance, with its "heathenish din", that gets into the popular press as typical of African religion.

The doctors may denounce the witches by name, though they may avoid doing so unless they are sure that the people are unpopular. In some places the suspects are made to pass behind the witch-doctor, who watches them in a mirror and claims to be able to tell the true witches from their reflection. This is a variation of the scrying in water.

The doctor aims not only at curing the bewitched, but also at purging the witches themselves. At times accused persons have been killed, or hounded on to another village. But the doctor may undertake to break their power, and this consists chiefly in extorting a confession which is supposed to break the power of witchcraft by bringing it into the light of day. Then the accused are washed with medicines and restored to their families.

The bewitched person's soul is supposed to have been abstracted, and if the doctor can make a successful show of discovering it then the patient may be convinced of recovery. The doctors are not deliberate deceivers, it is all for the good of the patient, and no doubt they do restore hope to sick people, especially to the mentally sick.

SPIRITUAL FORCES

CHAPTER X

MAGIC AND SORCERY

Magic

THE African magician believes that there are vital forces, or spiritual powers, that he can tap. His work is not merely mechanical, but dependent upon spiritual belief. Hence magic can properly be said to come within the scope of religion. It is sometimes said that "magic commands, religion implores", because in the higher forms of religion men have to do with personal powers whose will is independent of and greater than man's. But the magician still believes that the powers he utilizes are spiritual, even if lower in the hierarchy of forces than are the gods.

Some writers on African affairs would retain the old word "fetish" for the magical objects used. But, as already pointed out in an earlier chapter, this word has the disadvantage of being used only of African magic, whereas African magical practices can be paralleled in almost every corner of the earth. We can better use words such as medicines, charms, amulets, talismans and mascots for African magical objects.

Both magic and medicine are spoken of at times in almost the same way. The former word is traditional and still widely used, but it has the disadvantage of suggesting miracle-working. The latter suggests association only with material medical means of healing. In African thought material and spiritual are almost indistinguishable. Hence the distinction of magic and medicine is difficult to make, and the two words can both be used, provided that their wide connotation is borne in mind.

Frazer's distinction of Homoeopathic and Contagious Magic is helpful. Homoeopathic magic works on the principle that like produces like, and one might quote endless examples from African life. In rain-making rites water is spewed into the air to make rain fall by imitation, or clouds of smoke are made to rise to help the clouds gather round. A woman may wear a doll in the hope of reproducing a child that she has lost, or a twin will wear an image of a dead twin. In sickness, spots may be pasted on the skin of a sufferer from a rash, and then washed off again. In hunting, images may be made of the game, with the idea of attracting it. This works in a negative way too, whereby people must avoid actions that would hinder the similarity working. A hunter's wife must remain chaste while he is away, lest evil befall him. The many taboos on blood, especially women's, are because they are thought to cause harm.

Contagious magic is based on the notion that things once joined must remain so and can affect one another. Harmful charms can be made of a man's waste hair, nails, clothing, bath water, sleeping-mat, and anything that is his. So chiefs walk about with a servant carrying a spittoon, lest the chief's spittle be left on the ground and used by an evil magician. The placenta and navel cord of babies are carefully buried, so that they may not be used for a harmful purpose. Nurses sell these from hospitals at a high price to anxious parents.

One may distinguish Personal from Public Magic. A great many charms are individual, meant for specific needs of one person. Many of them are mixtures of leaves stuffed into horns, gourds, or leather packets, which the owner wears. Men wear teeth of animals, magic miniature scissors and knives, caps to make them invisible or safe against attacks of animals. Guns have their own medicine, and one notices that the old muzzle-loading flint-locks (Dane guns), which are still used, are loaded with protective magic for they are liable to explode or not go off at the needful moment. Modern guns often have no medicine at all for they are efficient in themselves.

Men wear charms in their hair, armlets of iron or leather, bracelets of tinkling metal, girdles laden with leather pouches, anklets of metal. Most common are rings against snakes and scorpions. Finger-rings and ear-rings have frequently a magical as well as an ornamental value. Many of the leather packets worn by modern Africans contain texts from the Koran or the Bible. Even in towns people have these stuffed in their pockets.

Public magic is seen in the charms used to protect houses, compounds, fields and villages. One sees bundles of feathers, bunches of leaves, packets wrapped in cotton thread, or great parcels hanging from the ceilings of rooms to protect their occupants. Shops have packages or magic brooms nailed above the door, to repel burglars or attract trade. Fields are protected by anything from a wisp of straw to a complex package containing teeth, blood, feathers and other dynamic substances. These are often the most obvious signs of paganism to the casual observer.

Many West African villages are entered through a protecting arch, which is supposed to remove all evil from those who pass under it. Disease is held to be excluded by the same means, and it is assumed that the evil spirit will come along the path and not through the bush. Men seem to think that they can outwit spiritual beings.

Thonga doctors in South Africa make magical fences round villages. One description of the medicine used for this purpose runs as follows: "a kind of ointment in which are contained different powders made up of various sea-animals, the jellyfish . . . the sea-urchin, the sponge and others. To these sea-animals are added some roots which have been exposed to the light by the rain which has washed out the soil in the kloof. All the drugs, which are also used to obtain rain, are mixed with fat and burnt on charcoal at dawn on the road to the village to protect the main entrance. Stones are daubed with it and put in all directions to close other openings. Then a second fire is made before the threshold of the hut and the smoke which comes out from the magical fat will keep the *baloyi* (sorcerers) away for fear of being revealed."[1] The magic works through objects that have been removed from hiding in the sea and under the ground, and thus they threaten sorcerers with similar exposure.

When men go to live in the modern towns, mines and ports of Africa they still use many magical charms. Indeed, while the ancient gods may decline, the practice of magic seems to remain as strong as ever. In the bewildering conditions of the towns men need spiritual powers to support them. These are partly provided by the new religions, but also backed up by new charms. New situations demand new medicines. These are provided both by the old medicine-men, who flourish in the

[1] H. A. Junod, quoted in *Bantu-speaking Tribes of South Africa*, p. 234.

towns, and also by new medicines, the quackery of Europe and India. Many European and Asian charlatans do a great export trade of magical objects to Africa. Almost every day I read in my morning Nigerian paper advertisements for Chinese Good Luck Rings, Mesmerism Charms, Kavachas Seals, Gocifuge Candles, Oriental Incense, Hindu Occult Art Magic, Wonder-working Prayers, Egyptian Secrets, Moses' Higher Mysteries, Greater Key of Solomon, etc. These trumperies are sold at anything from 2s. 6d. to 95s.

Most of the charms men wear, and the magical medicines they use, appear pathetically useless. But men do not invent them for the fun of the thing, as the European charlatan may do, but to meet some real need. Most African medicine-men are sincerely anxious to effect a cure, or to establish a protective influence over a village. I should like to quote again, as I have done elsewhere, the kindly words of Rattray. "The labour and infinite pains, the prayers, the spells, the sacrifices, the abnegation, the heart-burning, the disappointments, the hopes that are inseparably bound up in each of these poor fetishes we can only imagine in part, but they should never be quite lost sight of when we are considering such objects, or judging the makers of them."[1]

"Black Magic" and Sorcery

Magic is offensive as well as protective, and the former type passes under various names. The term "black magic" has not only been used in Europe to describe the harmful variety, it is also found in different parts of Africa. In the Gold Coast medicines which have worked well are congratulated by being smeared with whitewash, while those which work in the dark are blackened with charcoal. The Zulu distinguish between "black medicines" which are very strong or purge away the blackness of evil, and "white medicines" which soothe and purify.

Offensive or "black" magic is much feared, and many charms are worn with the object of defeating it by the use of a stronger power. Babies are loaded with bracelets and charms to protect them from evil influences and witchcraft. Lovers protect

[1] *Religion and Art in Ashanti*, pp. 21-2.

themselves against their rivals or jealous husbands. Farmers and blacksmiths arm themselves against accidents with their tools which may have been caused by sorcerers. Rings are worn against snakes sent by evil men.

The good, or "white", protective medicines are prepared by qualified medicine-men. They are made by an expert, who knows how to manipulate the forces that make them effective. As already stressed, the medicine-man or diviner is a respected figure in village life, he is consulted by nearly everyone and is well in the public eye.

The "black magician", sorcerer or wizard, on the other hand, is an evil person, feared and hated. He works in darkness, because his deeds are evil. The good medicine-man will not make harmful medicines; if he were to do so, many people think, his power would turn against him for it is a dangerous force. So those who wish to harm their enemies have resort at night and in secret to the sorcerer.

Many African peoples, but not all, make a distinction between the sorcerer and the witch. Both are feared, but their work differs. The name used for both may be the same, but they are often distinguished as "day-witch" and "night-witch". The "day witch", or sorcerer, is a conscious and deliberate evildoer; this is in contrast to the witch who works during sleep at night.

The sorcerer deliberately tries to harm his enemies, or those of clients who have paid him, by evil magical means. He may use suggestive magic only, or true poison. Harmful ingredients may be put in a cooking-pot or drinking-gourd. The sorcerer may put magical preparations secretly in a man's house, or lay a trail of powder round his hut. At the very sight of such powder men have been known to die. The soul of the enemy may be pinned down with pegs, or a clay image made of his body and thorns stuck in the vital organs. The enemy will then feel pain in those spots and may die. The sorcerer may utter spells and curses against his foe, or even threaten him openly in a quarrel. So men are careful not to offend one who is suspected of possessing evil powers.

All manner of evil, that might otherwise be called accidental or misfortune, is attributed to the maleficence of sorcerers:

broken limbs, cramp, internal pains, stillborn babies, twins, and any unusual events are taken as showing that sorcerers are on the warpath.

Sorcerers, like witches, may have animal familiars to work for them. Or they themselves may have the power of metamorphosis, and change themselves into animal form at will. Stories are widely told of sorcerers who change into birds or beasts of prey, leaving their mortal bodies asleep at home. If by good fortune someone succeeds in killing the animal during this period, then it will be found that the wizard has died at home at the same instant.

Sorcerers may send their animal agents against their foes. A snake or leopard can attack the enemy in the bush, and harm him even though he carries charms against such attack. That the charms are ineffective is taken as showing that some greater force is working against it. This serves as a useful explanation as to why charms may not act against wild animals. Similarly a sorcerer can call down lightning upon his victim, it is believed, or he may claim to rise up in the air himself and come down disguised as lightning. This belief in the ability of wizards to invoke the lightning is very common (as it was in Europe in the Middle Ages), and sceptics are told that their minds are not strong enough to understand such mysteries. It is, after all, but the reverse side of rain-making.

Sorcerers are believed, especially in East and South Africa, to be able to use men as their evil agents, and particularly the dead that they raise for their wicked purpose. Not only is the flesh of corpses sometimes used in bad medicines, but the dead themselves can be captured. "The witch beats the grave with a switch, and the grave opens and the body comes out. He drives a wooden splinter into the dead man's head so that he becomes foolish, and pierces his tongue with a long bone needle, so that he cannot speak. The raised person takes the form he had when alive."[1] The sorcerer then sends the ghost out to injure his enemies.

Other wizards are believed to have semi-human familiars that they control: small hairy beings, often with only one leg, who are very mischievous and adept at thieving and stealing

[1] M. Hunter, *Reaction to Conquest*, p. 289.

children. Sometimes the wizard makes a clay image of a demon, which is then supposed to inhabit it. The image is placed outside an enemy's house, or at a crossroads where many people pass. One man told me that he was able to send such a demon a hundred miles to fetch his enemy who would be chased back running all the way, and would return within the hour.

Divination

Divination or augury, foretelling the future by magical acts, is very popular in Africa. Geomancy, divining by figures on the earth, is found throughout the continent. One writer has traced it from Senegal to Madagascar. Divination is not only a means of discovering things to come, but is also used to uncover past secrets, and to smell out witches and sorcerers.

There are many different systems of divination in vogue. The Thonga of Mozambique use six half-shells of a fruit, three being male and three female. The shells are thrown on to a mat by a diviner, and the way in which they fall indicates success or failure. If the convex side of the shell falls uppermost the augury is favourable, but if the concave side shows up the omen is bad. Combinations of the sides of the different shells give complex messages. If the whole group is unfavourable another try may be made, on due payment of fees. Neighbouring tribes use a wooden bowl in which the shells float in water containing medicines. Round the edge of the bowl are carved symbols of the life and activity of the tribe.

Other peoples, such as the Basuto, use pieces of carved ivory or dice. The Basuto divination set is made up of four principal bones and a number of accessories. Two bones are male and are decorated so that the fall of each one can be interpreted in four ways. Two bones are female and each can be interpreted in two ways. The four bones together can make up sixty-four different combinations, and further permutations are possible with the other objects. Some other tribes have sixteen bones, representing the grades of people in tribal life.

There are most complex divinatory systems in West Africa. A number of different types of divination are used, from water-gazing to casting strings of bones and nuts. But the most developed is the Ifa system of the Yoruba of Nigeria, which has proved so fascinating that it has spread far to the east and west of its traditional home.

I have twice described this system in other books, but a few points may be mentioned here. One is the use of convex and concave nuts. Another is the basic figure four, with its multiples 16, and 256 and even 4,096. Then there is the use of written signs, marked on a board, which is the only instance of writing practised before modern times among the pagan and non-Islamic peoples.

Two principal methods are used in the Ifa divinatory system. One is by a cord which has four nuts strung on either end. This is thrown on to the ground, and the interpretation is given according to how many of the nuts present convex or concave surfaces. This easy system is used by diviners on their own behalf every day and for simple consultations by clients.

In the more complex system the diviner uses a wooden board, round or rectangular, along the edges of which are carved mythical figures. The board is sprinkled with powder in which the diviner makes marks. He sits by the board and holds sixteen palm nuts in one hand. He passes them rapidly to his other hand, and makes a stroke on the board according to the number of nuts left in his hand. If two nuts are left he marks one stroke in the powder, if one nut is left he marks two parallel strokes. If more than two, or none at all, are left then that turn does not count and he tries again. This process is repeated eight times, until there is a figure formed of two double columns of four groups of strokes, either single or double.

The interpretation of this system, as of the similar one with the cord, follows a highly involved tradition of verses and legends. As there are at least 256 combinations possible from any one act of divination, either on the simpler or more intricate system, there is a considerable feat of memory in the interpretation.

Men consult diviners on many occasions, and they are among the most popular and busy figures in religious life. If anything is lost, if a barren woman desires children, if there is a mysterious disease, if a man is troubled by strange dreams, and for many other causes, the diviner is sought out and he has recourse to his geomancy. The diviner may be called in at all the important crises of life; at birth to discover the appropriate name to give to a child, at betrothal to find the right husband, at death to find who has caused death. In some places the diviner draws up a horoscope for adolescents, and this is treasured by them for the rest of their lives as showing their fate. The horoscope is inscribed on a piece of calabash, and any competent diviner should be able to read it.

Other methods are used of consulting oracles. Water-gazing is common, but not crystal-gazing. A bowl is filled with water, in which are frequently placed medicines, cowrie shells, stones and beads. The diviner gazes fixedly into the water, and either thinks he sees the face of the guilty person appear, or else draws deductions as to his identity from the way in which the objects in the bowl are disposed.

Ordeals are supposed to indicate the guilt or innocence of the accused. Formerly practised with poisons which had to be drunk or vomited by the accused, they are now often administered to fowls who act as substitutes. The poison may be fatal, and the way in which the dead fowl lies on the ground is significant in showing guilt or innocence. The spiritualistic seance is also used to obtain guidance about unknown matters, but more of this later. "Carrying the corpse" is widely done to discover if anyone in the village is the cause of death, in which case the corpse is supposed to stop by the guilty one. Examination of entrails, of animals and of suspected witches, may also be done to determine the unknown.

Of all these methods there is no doubt that the manipulation of bones and nuts, with their complex interpretation, is the most sophisticated. One authority says, "The art (of bone-throwing) is so perfect that bone-throwers can find any amount of satisfaction in practising it. Consider that, in fact, all the elements of Native life are represented by the objects contained in the basket of divinatory bones. It is a *résumé* of all their social order, of all their institutions, and the bones, when they fall, provide them with instantaneous photographs of all that can happen to them. This system is so elaborate that I do not hesitate to say that . . . it is the most intelligent product of their psychic life."[1]

[1] H. A. Junod, *The Life of a South African Tribe*, vol. ii, pp. 521-3.

On these divinatory systems a great deal of care and thought is expended. The fascination of numbers has gripped these minds. But do they draw useful conclusions from them? The same writer continues: "If this system of divination is a token of great intelligence, its results, in the psychic life of the tribe, are most deplorable . . . I am convinced that, whatever may be the astuteness engendered by the divinatory bones, they have been extremely detrimental to the intellectual and moral welfare of the Natives."

The time and interest spent on these divinatory systems is very great, and appears out of all proportion to what truth such haphazard methods may reveal. It is hard to believe that the chance throws of bones or nuts can reveal the past or uncover the future. From my own experience I would trace the true wisdom not to the divinatory system, but to the wide experience, the keen perceptiveness and the deep intuition of the diviner himself. There is undoubtedly some degree of telepathy and extra-sensory perception at work at times. The great popularity of the diviner shows that he has a leading function to perform in society, and this he does as mediator and guide in many a quarrel, trouble and sickness.

CHAPTER XI

WITCHCRAFT

What is a Witch?
THE confusion that has been constantly noted over the names of people and practices in African spiritual life, is to be observed again in speaking of witchcraft. Witchcraft is frequently mistaken for magical practices and sorcery, just as a witch-doctor has been confounded with a priest or even with witches themselves.

It is important to distinguish the witch from the magician or sorcerer. And since most witches are believed to be women, the word witch can equally well serve for men. A "wizard" may then be taken as another name for a sorcerer, as the *Oxford*

Dictionary allows, and the title "witch" reserved for both men and women who are accused of nocturnal preying on human souls.

This distinction is to be found in many African languages, or if the names themselves are not distinct then a differentiation is often made in practice. Thus in Bechuanaland people distinguish "night witches" from "day sorcerers". The former are old women who fly about at night with other old crones and animal familiars. The latter live in solitude, are mostly male, and use tangible medicines for harming their enemies by day or night.

Professor Evans-Pritchard, whose epoch-making work on witchcraft has changed the tone of all studies of the subject, says that "Azande distinguish clearly between witches and sorcerers. Against both they employ diviners, oracles and medicine." They think that witches injure them by an inherent quality rather than by bad medicine, whereas sorcerers make people ill by performing magic rites.[1]

Some South African peoples have one word that they use for both witches and sorcerers, but at times it is qualified with other words to indicate the difference between night-witchcraft and day-witchcraft. To all, witchcraft is an evil thing, it is often hereditary, many of its practitioners are women. All kinds of trouble may be caused by witchcraft, from barrenness in human beings to a bad harvest. Always the help of a witch-doctor of some type will be sought, so that he may combat the evil by his superior power. Some peoples, in South and East Africa, seem to have merged the concepts of witchcraft and sorcery into one, but many of the characteristic features of witchcraft belief remain.

West African beliefs show the same distinction of witchcraft from sorcery. The work of witches is similar to that of other parts of Africa, with minor variations. Whereas sorcerers use magical medicines to do their evil work, the witches have no palpable apparatus of their trade, and their activities may properly be described as spiritual. They are secret agents, and are not consulted by men anxious to harm their enemies as sorcerers are consulted.

[1]*Witchcraft, Oracles and Magic among the Azande*, p. 21.

The activities of Witches

What is said in this chapter is based on popular African beliefs in what witches are and do, and in describing witchcraft I do not intend to commit myself to belief in the reality of it. There is no cult of witchcraft, and the popular theory that European witchcraft developed out of pagan ritual finds no counterpart in Africa.

How does one become a witch? It is widely believed that witchcraft is hereditary. Many African peoples think that all or most witches are women, and that the mother passes down her witchcraft to her daughter, but it is not inherited by her sons. At the same time it will be only latent in the girl till she has passed puberty, and it is rare to hear of a child witch. Some are born witches, others acquire witchcraft. In the Gold Coast it is believed that witchcraft may be bought for a small sum, or be obtained from demons or the dead. Others think of it as an infection that can be taken with food, and the recipient then gets a craving for human flesh.

The Azande believe in a witchcraft-substance which is found in the body of witches. Their ideas are rather vague, but they think of it as a blackish swelling, which may be the gall-bladder or part of the small intestine. If an accused witch dies then a post-mortem is held to try to find the witchcraft-substance. If it is found the intestines are strung out on a tree, but if not then the body is properly buried. This witchcraft is inherited from parents, both male and female, but the power may not always be used and so not be dangerous. When the bewitching power is felt to be active men do not ask the oracles who are the village witches, for there may be many, but they ask who is exercising his witchcraft power.

Most African peoples believe the majority of witches, or even all of them, to be women. The Nupe of Nigeria think that men also can be witches, but they are not so dangerous as the female of the species. The significance of this will be discussed again when considering the social setting of witchcraft.

Witchcraft is a social activity, like the sabbaths and covens in which medieval Europeans believed. The witch may be an old crone, living in solitude, or suspect by her family, but at night she is thought to join her fellows and carouse together.

They are often thought to be organized into a company, with a fixed number of members, strict rules for admission, and officials who perform the leading actions.

At the same time these witch meetings are spiritual. Witchcraft is an activity of the soul. There is no sound evidence yet available to show that any physical meeting of witches ever takes place. This is a bold statement, but it becomes clear after reading all the evidence available. The principle behind all witchcraft belief is that the witch sends out her soul, to prey on other sleeping souls, and to meet with fellow-witches in some remote place. It is generally believed that the witch's body remains on her bed while she is absent. Sometimes it is thought that the witch's soul travels along a cobweb to her meeting. Always it is held that if anything prevents the return of her soul, her body will perish.

Witches are believed to be conscious of their meetings, and to know and recognize their fellow witches. But it is exceedingly difficult to discover whether accused women actually do believe that they have met with others. They may confess or deny it, but that gives no certain proof. Some witches may claim to be able to recognize others during the day-time, and the witch-doctor pretends to have this power, though it may only be available to him when in a trance.

Witchcraft is nocturnal. The witch is supposed only to go out at night, and during the sleep of her body. She preys on other souls that are wandering while their bodies are asleep. Since people believe that dreams are the activities of the soul, which travels to the places the dreamer thinks about and meets the people he sees in the dream, it is not hard to see that a great deal of witchcraft belief depends on dreams.

Witches fly through the air to their meetings. The belief in their flight is as strong in Africa as it was in ancient Europe. In some places witches are thought to fly as balls of fire. The cry of birds may be taken as their signal for assembly, or mystical drums may be beaten to call them together. Then the whole company will flock together from different directions.

Witches have animal familars with which they work in close contact. Some people believe that they fly to the assembly mounted on the backs of owls, antelopes, leopards or nocturnal birds. The night birds are the commonest associates of witches: night-jars, owls, bats and fireflies. Black cats and snakes are also popular. Other people think that the witches turn into animals, and so fly away in disguise; to kill the animal is to destroy the witch.

Since witches fly with birds or swift nocturnal animals, it is not surprising that their favourite haunts are in the tops of trees. Tall trees in the forest, or hollow or curiously-shaped trees, like the baobab, are widely held to be the meeting-places of witches. Do not bats and owls lodge there?

The chief purpose of witch's meetings is spiritual cannibalism. The accusation was made of European witches that they devoured tender babes in their Sabbath. This accusation is made so realistically, and confessed to, in modern Africa that one feels there must be some physical cannibalism behind it. The witches are charged each to provide a victim in turn, and their meeting is a feast at which the various members of the body are devoured.

Yet it is quite clear that a spiritual eating is what is intended. Azande are sure that both the assembly and the feast of the witches are spiritual. They devour "the soul of the flesh". Similarly the Ibo of Nigeria believe that contributions are made to the witches' guild of the soul-substance of human victims. It all depends on the doctrine of souls, to which we come in the next chapter. Just as the witch goes in her own soul to the assembly, so she steals the soul of another person and carries it off to her companions.

The soul is eaten spiritually (to underline the obvious). That is to say, that although descriptions of the feast sound like cannibalism, yet it is spiritual. The assembled ghouls tear the victim limb from limb, eat it raw or cook it. Or the blood may be sucked, vampire-fashion. Yet all this is done to the soul and not the body. There are a few places where witches are said to dig up corpses, but this is not the general African belief. Such necrophagy is the work of sorcerers, who need dead bodies to provide powerful ingredients for their evil potions.

The soul is closely linked to the body, and as the witches devour the "spiritual body", so the mortal frame weakens. Its blood is sucked away spiritually. Pains, paralysis or impotence appear in different members. When the centre of blood, the heart or liver, is reached then the victim dies. One of the main tasks of the witch-doctor is to discover what the witches have done with the soul of his patient. If they have hidden it, he uses his medicine to recover the lost member. If he catches a witch, he will force her to confess what she has done with the soul, and to surrender her witchcraft powers.

The victims brought to the assembly are mostly close relatives. Witchcraft acts most often upon those who are in close contact with the witches. The new witch entering the company must bring the soul of a relative, often one of her own children. This sounds horrible, but the simple explanation may be in the excessive child mortality through disease. If the witch does not find a victim she is liable to be torn to pieces by the other enraged harpies.

Witch-hunting

Something has already been said as to the way in which witchcraft is counteracted, in the description given of witch-doctors and their training. Many methods are in use in Africa, and most diviners practise witch-finding as a regular part of their job. The witch-doctors may detect the witches by going into trance, by using medicines, gazing into water, consulting the dead, and many other ways.

Accused witches are often made to submit to an ordeal to test their guilt or innocence. This may consist of some semi-poisonous matter to be swallowed. Today the poison may be administered to a fowl. The poison oracle is still widely used, and its decisions are respected by native law.

Smellers-out may be organized into groups who go from house to house or tour the countryside. Large numbers of people are rounded up for interrogation, and made to pass through the traditional ordeal if accused. There are many modern witch-hunting companies, who combine old and new methods to track out witches. Witchcraft is still very much feared in all parts of Africa, and so men adapt old ways to new circumstances, and enter modern towns as well as old villages to hunt out the soul-eaters.

In recent years there have been numerous new witch-finding movements in different parts of Africa. One was the Bamucapi which in 1934 spread across Nyasaland, Southern and Northern Rhodesia and into the Belgian Congo. The Bamucapi were young men in European clothing who travelled about in twos and threes smelling out witches. They would get the village chiefs to line all the people up in a row, men separately from women, and as they passed by they tried to catch their reflections in small mirrors. The mirror was supposed to reveal the witch. Anyone who refused to pass, or hid himself, was threatened with sickness and exposure.

The accused witches had to drink a reddish soapy medicine out of bottles. Protective charms were sold in small cloth bags, against all sorts of evils. The witches also had to surrender their horn of witchcraft, and if they denied having any their houses would be searched. As most people carry medicines in horns they are abundant. Great piles of horns were surrendered, and were supposed to contain evil medicines and human bones, but competent investigators failed to discover more than a very small proportion, less than ten per cent, of the supposed witches' medicines that might have been used for offensive magic.

The Bamucapi used modern methods, mirrors, medicines in bottles, and new types of treatment. They preached sermons in which they claimed that their founder, a certain Kamwende, had been raised from the dead paralysed down one side but having gained the secret of the new anti-witchcraft medicine. They expected him to return in a second coming. The movement opposed the Christian missions, despite its garbled semi-Christian ideas.

Another movement spread across West Africa after the Second World War. It came from the northern Gold Coast to the south, then eastwards to Togo, Dahomey, and eventually Nigeria where it enjoyed considerable vogue until prohibited by the government in 1951. This movement came to be known as Atinga, a perverted form of the original name Nana Tongo. The Antiga witch-finders, like the Bamucapi, called village chiefs to assemble the people. They cleared a space round a tree, built an altar of earth, and danced while others beat drums. During the dancing they went into trance and claimed to be able to detect witches. They initiated local people into the dancing.

The Atinga made a preparation of blood, water and kola nuts which the accused, all women, had to drink. Small pieces of the nuts were also sold as protection against witchcraft. The accused women had to surrender the tools of their trade. The chief one was supposed to be a pot of witchcraft containing the witches' familiar bird. Many pots and calabashes were surrendered, but observers never saw a bird or model of one. As pots and calabashes are innumerable anything could be handed in. Many women seized charms and images of gods and gave them up. Some of these were salvaged and put in local museums; they have nothing to do with witchcraft.

A woman who refused to confess was made to pass through an ordeal. She had to bring a fowl, some gin and money. The gin was poured on the altar, and the fowl had its throat half severed. It would run about and finally collapse, the way in which it lay showing guilt or innocence. If it fell on its back with breast upwards that was proof of innocence. If the ordeal was unfavourable the first time that woman could try again, on payment of fees. Most women confessed, some willingly, some under threats. A few were beaten to death for their obdurate protestations of innocence.

The secrets of the Atinga could be purchased, for large sums. When the movement was finally banned those who had bought the secrets were very annoyed, as were the villages that had not been visited by the cleansers. Bands of young men still roamed the villages, smashing temples of the old and rather discredited gods, but respecting the still venerated ancestral shrines. Both of these movements are notable for the prominence of youths, with modern ideas.

Some of the secret societies have a function in disclosing witches. There is a society in the Nupe and Yoruba country of Nigeria, which is represented by masqueraders covered with a cylindrical tent, anything up to fifteen feet high. These figures appear in the streets of towns and villages, dance during the day, and in the evening visit the corners of compounds looking for witches. They bend their great height over terrified women, and in the past the accused would be rushed into the bush and passed through an ordeal, if not beaten to death. The woman was made to dig the soil with her bare hands till the blood came, the appearance of blood was taken as proof of guilt. Even today women may be ill-treated and chased out of the village. Another society uses a bull-roarer, a strip of wood on the end of a cord which makes an eerie sound when twirled in the air. I have heard them chasing suspected witches from one place to another.

Not only pagans but some of the semi-Christian sects practise witch-finding. The Zionist prophets among the Zulu regularly seek out witches, so do the Seraphim in Nigeria. They preach, quote the Bible, and administer medicine, often ashes which are stuffed down the throat of the accused. No healing is complete until the horn of witchcraft is surrendered. Other more orthodox priests sing hymns and pray over bewitched persons, sprinkling with holy water and invoking the name of the Trinity. I have found one temple that uses the Tetragrammaton, the four consonants of Jehovah, inscribed in Hebrew characters on their notice-board; this name was used in medieval exorcism. So the new religions seek to meet the old needs. As long as witchcraft is so profoundly believed in, so long will men use all means available to combat it.

Confessions of Witches

In some parts of Africa witches confess freely to witch-craft, as many witches did in ancient Europe. This phenomenon is puzzling to the European observer, who cannot see any clear proof that the accused did really engage in bewitching. Then one remembers the confessions extorted from prisoners in Nazi and Communist trials, in twentieth-century Europe.

Dr. Field has recorded many confessions made by women accused of witchcraft in the Gold Coast. She examined over four hundred accused persons, and listened to their admissions when arraigned before the village authorities. Some of these confessions are detailed and intimate. Witches confessed to having met in assemblies but, Dr. Field concludes, whether they actually met or not "*I do not know.*"

One supposed witch said, "I am the mother of the child who is now sick. Our company have eaten the body. They gave me my daughter's heart to eat, but I did not eat it, and returned it to my daughter." Another said that the whole company had by now devoured all the members of the victim, "We have already distributed the parts of the child and have used them, so there is no remedy now."[1] Yet everyone present knew that the sick child in question still had its body intact; it was the spiritual body that had been eaten.

The Azande do not confess to witchcraft usually. They believe that witches are conscious and deliberate agents, and know that they have the power of witchcraft which they share with their cronies. But when a man is accused of witchcraft he has had no consciousness of being a witch, and he does not know who are the other witches. So he thinks of himself as an exception. But since the poison oracle has denounced him, he submits to its superior knowledge and undergoes the ritual cleansing. In this case, at least, the notions about witches' activities cannot come from the accused, but are derived from the current and traditional beliefs of society. Elsewhere, too, a great deal that is supposedly confessed comes from leading questions put to the accused.

There may be some other roots of witchcraft belief in addition to the questions and confessions. Dreams are important in this study. It is likely that people confess to witchcraft because they fear that they may have done what they are accused of while they are asleep, unconsciously and in ignorance. They may suffer from anxiety-dreams, and repressed feelings of hatred, and feel that their soul has visited their rival or enemy in reality.

The Social Significance of Witchcraft

Witchcraft is a social, or rather anti-social, phenomenon. Not only are witches supposed to act against society, but certain types of people are accused. It is important to try to find out why some are suspect and not others.

Women are the most prone to suspicion of witchcraft. In some parts of Africa all witches are believed to be female, and in others the most dangerous are. The male role is to combat witchcraft, and keep women in subjection. A female witch-

[1]*Religion and Medicine of the Gã People*, p. 142.

doctor is a great rarity. The secret societies are concerned with male prestige, the preparation of adolescent boys, and the subjection of predatory female witches. The same predominance of women was noticeable in European witchcraft. The antagonism of the sexes is an important factor in the belief.

Kinship stresses are other roots of witchcraft. Witchcraft is rarely feared from people far away, but chiefly from those near at hand. "A man's foes shall be they of his own household." The mother-in-law conflict is prominent. Young wives denounce their husband's mother, or another wife in the polygamous household. The wife is often a stranger in the family, having been married from another clan or village. If she has no children she may be suspected of jealousy. Even more if her own children die she may be accused of having killed them. Or she will accuse a barren woman, a co-wife, or a mother-in-law past the age of bearing, of jealousy and child-murder by witchcraft.

The high rate of infant mortality favours these suspicions, and old midwives are frequently impeached. A medieval inquisitor said that midwives are the chief foes of the Church. In witchcraft accusations the husband will rarely succour an accused wife, for he may have several wives or be kept back by his mother. But a son will rally more quickly to his mother's side, and at times defend her with success.

No doubt there are awkward and unsociable people too, who are easily suspect. There are neurotics, in Africa as elsewhere, who are a prey to jealousies and fears, and who confess in order to obtain release from their complexes. Perhaps some of these people may utter spells against their neighbours at times or drop poison in their soup, but this is sorcery and different from what they are accused of doing in witchcraft. More significant are the suppressed desires, the unuttered jealousies, the veiled hatred, which project themselves only in evil imaginings. Women may confess to such spiritual malevolence, and believe that they have in very truth devoured the souls of their rivals.

The Future of Witchcraft

"Witchcraft is an imaginary offence because it is impossible," said Evans-Pritchard. "A witch cannot do what he is supposed to do and has no real existence. A sorcerer, on the other hand, may make magic to kill his neighbour."

Rare indeed is the African who will agree with the first sentence in the preceding paragraph. For witchcraft is still very widely feared, and apparently just as much under the influence of modern civilization and Christianity as ever before.

European governments have tried to legislate against witchcraft and witch-hunting. In doing so they have hindered the work of the witch-doctor himself, and so earned the scorn of Africans who regard the modern laws as a very encouragement to witchcraft because they oppose the work of witch-doctors. The Nigerian laws penalize those who claim to have the power of witchcraft; apparently not realizing that people do not claim to have this power except under accusation. In Uganda and Tanganyika witch-doctors and witch-finders are threatened with five years in prison. While in Kenya any person who pretends to exercise supernatural power is penalized. This might apply to a prophet or priest of any religion. How would Moses or Elisha fare in Kenya?

Governments have not clearly understood the nature of the thing with which they have to deal. Africans might well say that they have not "the right sort of eyes" to perceive witchcraft. But anthropologists and serious students maintain that witchcraft, as distinct from magic and sorcery, is illusory. It will be many years before their conclusions are accepted, but it must be said that their works are the only serious studies that have been made of the subject.

In modern African towns there is still great fear of witchcraft. The conditions of the time favour this. Witchcraft belief is an expression of social disease, and this is a time of exceptional unrest. In the towns men meet many strange forces, and strangers from other tribes who may have powerful evil forces at their disposal. To protect himself against misfortune, sickness, unemployment, lack of promotion, failure in examination, and all the ills of life, man has recourse to the diviner and witch-doctor.

There is some debate as to whether belief in witchcraft is

increasing or decreasing. Perhaps it is on the decline, relatively to other forces at work, education, hospitals, churches, and western ways of life and thought. Slowly new ideas are adopted. The old is tenacious, life is insecure, but there are forces of enlightenment that, it may be hoped, will release men from some of the fears with which they are beset.

CHAPTER XII

THE SOUL AND ITS DESTINY

AFRICAN ideas of the soul and spirit are very complex. This is not surprising when one considers that European teaching has also been confused. Shakespeare wrote of three souls. A recent philosopher identifies soul and spirit, distinguishes mind only as a temporary "by-product of the soul's incarnation in matter", and confesses that the interaction of mind with brain and body is a mystery.

The complexity of African ideas is so great that some peoples have beliefs in at least five distinguishable spiritual powers in man. Of others, as Dr. Edwin Smith says of some Rhodesians, "The soul as we speak of the soul, it is doubtful whether the Ba-ila believe in it. Certainly we have never found a word that would be a satisfactory translation." I have discussed some African ideas of the soul in my *West African Psychology*, and I make no pretence of having made an exhaustive study.

That there is a spiritual nature in man no African peoples doubt. In one aspect it is akin to what we call the personality of a man. It is identifiable with the ego, and is responsible for the peculiar characteristics of individuality. It helps to explain why people are different in face, why voices differ, why each has his own oddities.

This soul is a power, and some writers would approximate it to the vital forces in the universe, rather than to a personal spirit. As a kind of soul-stuff it animates the body, pervading it with life. When it is separated from the body, by witchcraft or death, then the body dies.

The soul is closely connected with the breath, for this is a clear accompaniment of vitality. It may be thought of as residing in the mouth and nose, and as going away at death. The heart, too, is a source of blood and life, and ceases beating at death; some people use the same word for heart as for soul. Then there is the shadow, which is akin to the breath and disappears at death. The conventional belief is that corpses cast no shadow and that is how one knows a ghost. Yet while breath and shadow vanish at death, and are not generally thought to live on elsewhere, the personality may hover around the grave for some time or be reborn into the family in a new-born child.

We have seen that people believe the soul to wander about in dreams. Care must be taken not to awaken a heavy sleeper suddenly, else his soul may not have returned to his body in time. Day-dreamers are said to have let their soul wander. The fact that dead people are seen in dreams is taken as a proof of their continued existence. If a man dreams frequently of his dead father he will take care to offer gifts at his grave, and consult a diviner to find out if his father has any special wishes.

Witches travelling about in spirit are believed to seize dreaming souls. Men feel this if they wake up in pain. Children who cry out in the night may be troubled by witches, and even cattle that behave strangely have perhaps been bewitched. For this reason men do their utmost to protect their souls against witches, and other workers of iniquity.

Sir James Frazer made much of an idea which be called "the external soul". His theory was that men believe the soul to be a manikin, identical with the physical body, and that they hide this soul in some external object, a pot or box, and go away leaving it in safety. If they are attacked without their soul they cannot be hurt fatally, the only danger would be if somebody discovered the soul in the box. This favourite hypothesis is much too concrete, and finds little support in most of Africa. Possibly some tribes of the Congo have comparable ideas. But the general belief is that those who can leave their bodies are sorcerers, who have the power of putting their souls in animals, in a kind of metamorphosis. If the animal is killed then the sorcerer dies.

Man has other spiritual forces associated with him. In West and East Africa there is a belief in a divine spirit, a guardian genius which overshadows or protects a man. This is not unlike Plato's belief in the sovereign part of the soul, which dwells at the top of the body and is given to each of us by God as a demon. It may be compared with Emerson's doctrine of an Oversoul, or the more general idea of a conscience, a spark of the divine within each man. This guardian genius gives good and bad fortune, like fate. It may offer advice in the low voice of conscience or if angered may be responsible, directly or indirectly, for an accident occurring to its ward.

Some people believe in spiritual relatives, heavenly twins of earthly souls, which guide and help their mortal counterparts. There are also tribal or clan spirits, totemic inheritances from the father or mother. These may best be understood in the setting of social relationships, without regarding them as separate souls.

Ghosts

At death the soul leaves the body. The time of leaving is estimated to be at the moment the last breath is drawn, or when earth is put on the corpse in the grave. The soul may still hang round the grave for a time, or be available there to receive gifts and consultations.

Some people think that the soul is now more fully personal, and less of a vague soul-stuff, than during the life of the body. But it is certainly still a complex entity. For not only may the deceased person be invoked at the graveside, but he also is thought to travel to the land of the dead, and in addition may be reincarnated on earth. The soul may therefore be bipartite or tripartite.

The dead are commonly supposed to go to a world under the ground, like Hades of the Greeks, where it is dark and cold. Some think there is water to be crossed, like the Styx. There are some Nigerian peoples who believe in heavens above, a "heaven of fresh breezes" for the good, and a "heaven of broken pots" for the bad. There is belief in judgement by God. The underworld idea is a natural conclusion from burial in the ground.

Here the spirit of the earth takes the dead into her pocket. The dead are often supposed to live a life like that on earth. Social distinctions may be preserved there, though some hold levelling theories.

In the underworld are the ancestors. The newcomer takes money, presents and food, to help him on his journey and to have something to offer his seniors when he arrives. Some time may elapse for the repose of the departed soul, then the ceremonies of "second burial" help it enter fully into the status of an ancestor.

The word "ghost" needs careful definition. Strictly, it should be used only for the apparition of departed spirits. The belief in a phantasm, an appearance of a dying or recently dead person, is different but is very common. Most circumstantial tales are told of such phantasmal visions. The phantasm usually appears when a man dies away from home, and it is visible to a close relative only. The dying person has sent out his soul, as in a dream, to visit his relative who will realize at once that the friend is dead.

A ghost is an apparition or spectre of a dead person. Ghosts of people who have been dead for some time are believed to appear, in dreams or in waking life, usually at night. They give messages to their living relatives, and diviners are consulted to discover or interpret the ghost's wishes. Some ghosts plague men and bring sickness to children. Then efforts are made to placate them, or drive them away with shouting, drumming and insults. The corpse may be dug up and the bones scattered, and this is thought to break the residual vital force of the ghost and render it harmless.

Some ghosts are the spectres of those who have not received proper burial, and they wander about seeking rest until the full rites of "second burial" are performed for them. Such are the ghosts of hunters who have been lost in the forest, fishermen drowned at sea, people burnt in a village fire or struck by lightning.

In South Africa some ghosts are believed to be seized by sorcerers for their wicked purposes. Their souls may be captured before death, or the corpses dug up and parts of the body extracted. The soul is then a slave to the sorcerer and is sent out by him on evil errands, to steal food or property, to make people sick or kill them. Sometimes they enter into and possess people, and cause them great pain. Such ghosts are driven off by diviners.

Reincarnation

It is not widely realized that Africans have as strong a belief in reincarnation as have Hindus and members of other religions, such as Buddhism and Jainism. Whatever the origin of the belief, perhaps the resemblance between a child and its parents or grandparents, the idea of the rebirth of the departed soul is firmly held in most of Africa.

African belief, however, differs from Indian in important ways. The notion of a round of existence, gripping all beings in cycles of rebirth, and from which men might escape only by great efforts to Nirvana, is quite lacking in African thought. Similarly the notion of reward or punishment being administered by rebirth into a higher or lower state, such as one finds in Plato as well as in Indian belief, is missing in Africa.

The Indian idea of this present world as a place of suffering and illusion is contrary to the African. The African thinks of this world as light, warm and living, to which the dead are only too glad to return from the underworld of darkness and cold. This is the best of all possible worlds; the African's attitude is world-affirming not world-renouncing. It is therefore a punishment to be detained in Hades, and childlessness is a curse because it blocks the channel of rebirth. All the dead return to the earth, except perhaps certain ghosts that have been captured by sorcerers. Rarely does one find any limit set to the number of reincarnations, speculation does not go so far.

There is a common myth in Africa that the number of souls and bodies is limited. At the beginning of creation only a fixed number was made. The next generation was compounded of bodies made of the clay of the previous one, hence the family resemblance. A variation on this is that the number of souls is limited, and as the body wears out the soul is equipped with a new body made for the purpose of his rebirth.

It is important to discover what ancestor is reborn in a child. The moment when the ancestral spirit enters the child may be taken to be at the time of conception, or the quickening in the womb, or even as late as birth. The reborn soul may be that of a paternal or maternal relative, according to the system of patrilineal or matrilineal inheritance in force in the clan. Great efforts are devoted to marriage arrangements to ensure that there is proper affinity, so that tradition may be followed and the ancestors reborn. The diviner may be called in at birth to declare which ancestor has come back, this is particularly important if the child does not clearly resemble anyone. The child may be given a name there and then, the same as that of the reborn ancestor.

There are subtleties and refinements that defy logical analysis. The same ancestral spirit may be reborn in more than one person; separate diviners may declare a grandfather to be reincarnate in cousins born about the same time. Further, the departed spirit may be at once reborn, and yet spoken of as in the world of the dead, and also receive offerings at the grave. Father Tempels says that we must not be too precise, or import categories which do not fit; all is explicable by the philosophy of forces. The ancestor does not create the child, God does that. Nor is it strictly the ancestral spirit that is reborn, but the child comes under his protecting influence and receives some of his vitality. The ancestral name is renewed in the family, and is a revitalized clan influence.

The idea of transmigration, or metempsychosis, which implies possible change into animal form, needs to be distinguished from normal reincarnation. Some people have such ideas. The Nankanse of the Gold Coast believe that certain clans are related to animals. Men of the leopard clan are called "leopard-rising fellows", because it is believed that at death they will appear to their sons as leopards. They never kill leopards, and if they find one dead they wrap it in a white cloth and bury it with the same honours as a human being. Similar ideas may be behind the honour shown to pythons and other beasts.

The most common belief in transmigration is that in the power of a sorcerer to assume the shape of an animal. Also comparable is the belief of the witch assuming the form of her familiar animal. It is not clear whether these are thought of as real animals selected for the purpose, and if so what happens to their own souls. For animals and plants also have souls, though they are lower in the hierarchy of forces than those of human beings.

The belief in transmigration, and the existence of taboo animals, may point to ancient ideas of totemism. But it is rare to find any totemistic cults in Africa, at all comparable with those of North America and Australia. As one writer says, "The animals are peculiarly apt symbols for the livingness—the immortality—of the ancestors." The very aggressiveness of the animals symbolizes the fierce sanctions of the ancestors as supports for moral values.

Spiritualism

The dead are consulted in seances comparable with those of modern Europe and America, or with that of the so-called "witch" of Endor.

The principal figure in the spiritualistic seance is the medium, about whose training something was said in a previous chapter. The medium has a "control", that is to say a spirit that possesses her. The spirit may be a dead person, a divine being, or even an animal. The medium may be only occasionally possessed, or under the regular control of one particular spirit.

The spirit may be thought to enter the head or chest of the medium, and make her prophesy. Interrogated by a priest or diviner she gives the name of the possessing spirit. Then some message is given; warning of the abundance of witches, predicting famine or drought, or demanding large sacrifices to the ancestors. At the medium's word a witch may be killed, or a number of cattle slaughtered.

The medium gives messages from the dead, demanding more attention from relatives. Or she may declare who has been responsible for death. Recourse to mediums is frequent in cases of mysterious death, and as death is unnatural mediums are busy people.

Diviners believe they can call up the dead directly, into a pot or by means of the divining-board. This is done for a special purpose, at the demand of relatives who have an inquiry to make, such as whether the ancestor is incarnate in a new-born child.

The time spent on ritual connected with the dead is considerable, and shows the profundity of African belief in the spiritual
world, and in the importance of the ancestors. The dead are
felt to be ever near, and no people have a greater consciousness
than Africans of the reality of the watching "cloud of witnesses".

EPILOGUE

GREAT changes have taken place in Africa in the last century. In the tropical areas colonial rule has only come during the past fifty or sixty years, since the conquest of the mosquito. In that brief period African peoples have been thrust through the social and educational changes that came to Europe over the centuries since the Renaissance and the Industrial Revolution.

These changes have inevitably altered the religious picture. Not only have social changes occurred, in new forms of government, and the migration of people to towns and mines, but new religions have appeared on the scene. Christianity and Islam have come as missionary religions, and have had considerable success in displacing much of the old faith. Their success has undoubtedly been much greater than it would have been in past centuries, because of the unsettlement of African society in our day. Christian missions have been much more successful in Africa in replacing the ancient faith than they have in India or China, because African religion was less organized.

Islam, which was established for centuries in North and North-east Africa, has taken advantage of modern means of communication and the imperial peace to spread southwards in East and West Africa. Christianity has come up from the sea and established itself firmly in West, East and South Africa. Where these two world missionary religions meet there is rivalry, and it cannot yet be decided which will be the dominant religion. In East Africa the conversion of Uganda to Christianity has checked the southward spread of Islam. In many parts of West Africa Islam seems to be gaining the majority, since it takes over old customs more easily than Christianity, but the issue is still far from being decided.

Does this mean that African traditional religion has disappeared, and has only an antiquarian interest? By no means. In

142

the innumerable villages of Africa the ancient religion is still held by millions of people. Some peoples have become largely Christian, like the Baganda; others, such as the Lovedu, have nearly all rejected Christianity. Even in the towns, and among those who have accepted the new religions, there is a great substratum of traditional beliefs which must never be left out of account in an assessment of religious life. The ancient ideas constantly reappear in the separatist Christian sects, and in the magical and witchcraft beliefs which most people still hold.

In the villages the conservatism of society strengthens the retention of the old faith. The new religions are disliked because they undermine old customs. The missions oppose whatever may be called "idolatry". They have often been against dancing, because of its association with licentious or fertility cults, and the possession of dancers by spirits. Polygamy has been opposed, so have cross-cousin marriages, inheritance of wives, exorbitant dowries and heavy drinking at weddings. The chiefs have regarded the missions as undermining their authority. Christians may refuse forced labour, Sunday courts, and annual village ceremonies. As educated people they may cease to prostrate themselves before the chief, or even to remove their shoes in his presence. If the chief's authority is attacked, men say, not only will it cause disorder on earth but the very foundations of nature will be overturned: crops will not grow, rain will not fall, women will not bear children.

On the other hand, it must be recognized that Christians often form the progressive elements in village life. They are the ones who listen to the advice of agricultural officers suggesting new methods of farming, they build new houses, wear European clothes, make graveyards outside the village, and lead in political life. Education, above all, has come from the churches, and educated Africans owe much to the missions. Many people do not realize that Africans who visit Europe for study are nearly all products of mission schools, and so are favourably disposed towards the church, unless they get soured by a colour-bar.

Islam has done little in education. It spreads from the top downwards, converting the chiefs, retaining polygamy, and adapting festivals and dances. But both Christianity and Islam are obliged to adapt themselves in some degree to village life. It is in villages that experiments have been made by the missions towards reforming initiation rites for young people and converted chiefs.

The industrial and urban revolution has broken upon Africa, sending multitudes to live in towns, and wrenching them away from their family gods. Nevertheless people often take their gods with them when they remove, as did Rachel. But the ancestors, who are so important in village life, remain there with the old people.

Magical practices, however, stand the strain of removal to town life and multiply to meet new circumstances. The same thing happened when African slaves were taken across to America. The gods, and even more the ancestors, were at a discount but magic survived in Voodoo and Obeah. The markets of modern African towns abound in magical objects of all kinds. New ones are imported from the quacks of Europe and Asia. Of course there are education, hospitals, and the new religions to give positive enlightenment and combat magic, but it will be long before there is a decline of superstition.

Educated people attribute to witchcraft their failures in work, or seek magical protection against new diseases. They may use new types of medicine, but of a magical kind. Many have recourse both to the medicine-man and to the European-trained doctor. The medicine-man serves as a link with the village ancestors. He may interpret a patient's sickness or nightmares as due to an angry ancestor who has been neglected and demands that money be sent home to make him offerings.

The new religions are a great help in town life, in providing communities into which any stranger may enter, and where he can meet on equal terms with people of other tribes. Universal religions make the transfer easier from village to town, and they serve useful social functions in giving a faith to live by and providing against insecurity. They help in unemployment, sickness and death. While they do disintegrate to some extent, they also seek to reintegrate society, "to destroy and to overthrow, to build and to plant".

In many places it is becoming the respectable thing to declare oneself a Christian or a Muslim; it shows that one is modern and educated. Three years ago I made a survey of the proportion of religions in the city of Ibadan. Figures supplied by the churches gave ten per cent of the population as Christian; I suggested that about twenty per cent might include adherents. A census taken since then shows that even more, just a third of the total, wish to be regarded as Christian. Muslims I put at anything up to half, in the complete lack of statistics; but the census shows that some sixty per cent put themselves down as Muslim. The number of confessed pagans in this modern town is not much more than seven per cent. But this does not mean that many people are not still pagan in outlook, and even in practice; vast crowds take part in the annual fire and fertility festival in honour of the hill goddess of the town.

Ancient customs are seen particularly in the Christian sects, the so-called "African churches" which divide Christendom more and more. One reads very little about these sects in mission literature, but they are a potent factor in the religious situation. In South Africa over 800 such sects have been listed. Even in Uganda or the Gold Coast, where the mission churches have been strongly entrenched, there is an increase of schism.

The reasons for schism are various. It has been commonly thought that polygamy was the root cause, but this is only so in a minority of cases. After the secession has taken place, however, polygamy is often permitted as an ancient practice not clearly prohibited in the Bible, except to bishops and deacons. One chief reason for separation has been the desire for independence of European control. Another has been the wish to retain ancient African customs. In Kenya the churches opposed the practice of female circumcision, and so independent churches and schools were founded which permitted its continuance.

Many of the sects oppose the use of medicines, African or European, but they rely on faith, holy water, sacred oils, ashes and incense. They impose ritual taboos, such as upon the use of alcohol and tobacco and the eating of pork. Their leaders dress in white, like priests of the old religion, and they give great place to ritual and dancing. Emotionalism and possession are common among the sectarian prophets. The prophets have visions, interpret dreams, and seek to drive away witches. All these spiritual needs seem to be neglected by the orthodox churches, but it will be seen that they have their roots in the ancient religious beliefs.

In the new religions the ancient African belief in a Supreme Being is taken up and enlarged. Belief in the nature gods is opposed by Christianity and Islam, though the gods may linger in saint-worship at Muslim tombs and in Christian cults. Most people still believe in spirits of the forests, hills and streams, even if they do not worship them. The ancestors may have their cult transmuted, but belief in the nearness of the dead is very strong. The large and ornate tombs, the long obituaries, and the popular memorial services and masses, testify to this. Christian workers may still call their children "father has returned". Witchcraft belief and magic, we have seen, flourish as ever.

Students of African society have felt deep concern at the rapidity of social and religious change in Africa. Some would have prohibited missions from doing their work, but the clock cannot be put back. Imperialism, trade and education are just as disturbing as the new religions and, unlike them, have little positive moral ideal to put in place of the old. C. K. Meek, an anthropologist who made a study of the Ibo of Nigeria after riots in 1929, concluded, "Some of the ethics will disappear with the old gods, but new gods will create new ethical values . . . It is a commonplace to say that magic worked well, but we cannot lightly discount the fact that diviners, witch-doctors and ministers of ordeals were frequently bribed to give a favourable or unfavourable decision."

The greatest danger in African religious life is that the old should disappear, without some new religious force to take its place. Unchecked individualism, self-seeking, corruption and materialism are the great enemies of modern Africa. Yet the past has been so thoroughly impregnated with religion and its ethics that it is difficult to see how an ordered society can be established without them. There is no doubt that God spoke in time past to men in Africa, and that African faith can be led upwards into African interpretations of the new religions. From these will come the new morality which will save society. I cannot do better in closing than to quote, as I have done elsewhere, a wise saying by Placide Tempels: "African paganism, the ancient African wisdom, aspires from the root of its soul towards the very soul of Christian spirituality."

BIBLIOGRAPHY

Ashton, H., *The Basuto*. 1952.

Basden, G. T., *Niger Ibos*. 1938.
Baumann, H., *Schöpfung und Urzeit des Menschen im Mythus der Afrikanischen Völker*. 1936.
Bleek, D. F., *The Naron: a Bushman Tribe of the Central Kalahari*. 1928.
Bryant, A. T., *The Zulu People*. 1929.
Busia, K. S., *The Position of the Chief in the Modern Political System of Ashanti*. 1951.

Childs, G. M., *Umbundu Kinship and Character*. 1949.
Cremer, J., *Les Bobo*. 1927.

Danquah, J. B., *The Akan Doctrine of God*. 1944.
Dieterlen, G., *Les Ames des Dogons*. 1941; *Notes sur la Religion Bambara*. 1951
Doke, C. M., *The Lambas of Northern Rhodesia*. 1931.
Driberg, J. H., *The Lango*. 1923; *People of the Small Arrow*. 1930.

Evans-Pritchard, E., *Witchcraft, Oracles and Magic among the Azande*. 1937; *The Nuer*. 1940.

Field, M. J., *Religion and Medicine of the Gā People*. 1937.
Fortes, M. J., *The Dynamics of Clanship among the Tallensi*. 1945.

Hayley, T. T. S., *The Anatomy of Lango Religion*. 1947.
Herskovits, M. J., *Dahomey*. 1938.
Hunter, M., *Reaction to Conquest*. 1936.

Junod, H. A., *The Life of a South African Tribe*. 2nd edn. 1927.

Kenyatta, J. *Facing Mount Kenya*, 1938.

Krige, E. J. and J. D., *The Realm of a Rain-Queen*. 1943.

Kuper, H., *An African Aristocracy: Rank among the Swazi*. 1947.

Labouret, H., *Les Tribus du Rameau Lobi*. 1931.

Leakey, A. B., *Mau Mau and the Kikuyu*. 1952.

Little, K., *The Mende of Sierra Leone*. 1951.

Lucas, J. O., *The Religion of the Yorubas*. 1948.

Luttig, H. G., *The Religious System and Social Organization of the Herero*. 1933.

Mair, L. P., *An African People in the Twentieth Century*. 1934.

Maupoil, B., *La Géomancie à l'ancienne Côte des Esclaves*. 1943.

McCulloch, M., *The Ovimbundu of Angola*. 1952.

Meek, C. K., *The Northern Tribes of Nigeria*. 1925; *Tribal Studies in Northern Nigeria*. 1931; *A Sudanese Kingdom*. 1931; *Law and Authority in a Nigerian Tribe*. 1937.

Meyerowitz, E. L. R., *The Sacred State of the Akan*. 1951.

Nadel, S. F., *A Black Byzantium*. 1942; *The Nuba*. 1947.

Parrinder, G., *West African Religion*. 1949; *West African Psychology*. 1951; *Religion in an African City*. 1953.

Rattray, R. S., *Ashanti*. 1923; *Religion and Art in Ashanti*. 1927. *Tribes of the Ashanti Hinterland*. 1932

Richards, A. I., *Hunger and Work in a Savage Tribe*. 1932.

Roscoe, J., *The Baganda*. 1911; *The Banyankole*. 1923.

Schapera, I., *The Khoisan Peoples of South Africa*. 1930; ed. *The Bantu-speaking Tribes of South Africa*. 1937.

Schebesta, P., *Les Pygmées du Congo Belge*. 1952.

Seligman, C. G., *Races of Africa*., 1930. *Pagan Tribes of the Nilotic Sudan*. 1932.

Smith, E. W., *Ila-speaking Peoples of Northern Rhodesia*. 1920; ed. *African Ideas of God*. 1950.

Soga, J. H., *The Ama-Xosa: Life and Customs*. 1931.

Spieth, J., *Die Religion der Eweer in Süd-Togo*. 1911.

Stayt, H. A., *The Bavenda*. 1931.

Talbot, P. A., *Life in Southern Nigeria*. 1923; *The Peoples of Southern Nigeria*. 1926.

Tauxier, L., *La Religion Bambara*. 1927; *Religion, Moeurs et Coutumes des Agnis de la Côte d'Ivoire*. 1932.

Tempels. P., *La Philosophie Bantoue*. 1945.

Wagner, G., *The Bantu of North Kavirondo*. 1949.

Weeks, J. H., *Among the Primitive Bakongo*. 1914.

Westermann, D., *Die Glidyi-Ewe in Togo*. 1935.

Willoughby, W. C., *The Soul of the Bantu*. 1928.

Young, T. C., *African Ways and Wisdom*. 1937.

Ethnographic Survey of Africa (International African Institute, 1950–1953): Western Africa, West Central Africa, East Central Africa, Southern Africa.

INDEX

A

Aggrey, J. K., 33
Akan, cp. Ashanti
altars, 37, 88 f.
ancestors, 16, 22 f., 24 f., 31, 37, 43, 48, 51, ch. v, 74, 76, 83, 87, 89, 99, 102, 137 f., 144, 146
Angola, 150
animals, 23, 44, 53, 59, 114, 118, 125, 139 f.
animatism, 21 f.
animism, 20 f., 24
Ashanti, 11, 20, 31 f., 33, 37, 39, 42, 45, 47 f., 50, 58, 63 f., 65, 70 f., 74, 76, 83, 86, 89, 93, 97
Ashton, H., 60, 149
Azande, 107 f., 123, 126, 131

B

Ba-ila, 36, 41, 64, 87, 134
Bamangwato, 71, 82, 87
Bantu, 11, 23, 43, 57, 67, 68
Barbot, J., 16, 17
Basden, G. T., 149
Basuto, 11, 36, 59, 84, 94, 95, 97, 119
Baumann, H., 40, 149
Bechuana, 9, 11, 33, 36, 78, 95, 123
birth, 63, 91 f.
Bleek, D. F., 149
blood, 72, 88, 126 f., 135
Bowdich, T. E., 70
Bosman, W., 14, 15
Bryant, A. T., 105, 149
bride-price, see dowry
Burton, R. F., 14, 62
Busia, K. A., 48, 149

C

Cameroons, 33, 50
cannibalism, 88, 126
charms, 22, 26, 93, 101, ch. x

chiefs, 11, 25, 28, 45, 62, ch. vi, 99, 143
children, 60, 91 f., 138 f.
Childs, G. M., 149
Christianity, 10, 12, 33 f., 36, 43, 48 f., 86, 88, 94, 96, 101, 128, 133, 142 f.
circumcision, 11, 94 f., 145
Congo, 16, 34 f., 41, 67, 128, 135
Cremer, J., 149

D

Dahomey, 11, 45 f., 51, 70, 74, 94, 102, 128
Danquah, J. B., 31, 149
death, 98 f., 107, 137
demons, 53, 103
Dieterlen, G., 149
disease, 106 f.
divination, 48, 119 f.
diviners, 37, 103 f., 107, 120 f., 140
Dogon, 37, 39, 41, 89
Doke, C. M., 149
dowry, 11, 98, 143
dreams, 27, 61, 131, 135, 144
Driberg, J. H., 64, 81, 106, 149
dynamism, 21, 26

E

earth spirit, 23, 33, 47 f., 54, 83, 93
Egypt, 13, 32, 44, 49, 67, 76
embalming, 76
Evans-Pritchard, E., 27, 107, 123, 133, 149
Ewe, 45 f., 48, 71

F

Farrow, S., 32
"fetish", 15 f., 21, 113
Field, M. J., 59, 130, 149

153